Creating Caring Classrooms

How to encourage students to communicate, create, and be compassionate of others

KATHLEEN GOULD LUNDY

LARRY SWARTZ

Pembroke Publishers Limited

*To our friend, David Booth, who has taught us that to teach is
to help and to help is to care*

© **2011 Pembroke Publishers**
538 Hood Road
Markham, Ontario, Canada L3R 3K9
www.pembrokepublishers.com

Distributed in the U.S. by Stenhouse Publishers
480 Congress Street
Portland, ME 04101
www.stenhouse.com

We acknowledge the financial support of the Government of Canada through the Book
Publishing Industry Development Program (BPIDP) for our publishing activities.

We acknowledge the assistance of the Government of Ontario through the Ontario
Media Development Corporation's Ontario Book Initiative.

Library and Archives Canada Cataloguing in Publication

Lundy, Kathleen Gould
    Creating caring classrooms : how to encourage students to communicate, create, and
be compassionate of others / Kathleen Gould Lundy & Larry Swartz.

 Includes bibliographical references and index.
Issued also in electronic format.
ISBN 978-1-55138-270-8

    1. Classroom environment. 2. Classroom management. 3. Interpersonal relations—
Study and teaching (Elementary). 4. Social skills—Study and teaching (Elementary). 5.
Teacher–student relationships. I. Swartz, Larry II. Title.

LB3013.L86 2011   372.1102'4   C2011-904795-0

eBook format ISBN 978-1-55138-832-8

Editor: Kate Revington
Cover Design: John Zehethofer
Typesetting: Jay Tee Graphics Ltd.

Printed and bound in Canada
9 8 7 6 5 4 3 2

MIX
Paper from
responsible sources
FSC® C004071

Contents

Introduction

Addressing the Bigger Picture

If we are to raise kids who can think and act ethically, we don't begin with the thinking or the acting. We begin with caring.
—From *Just Because It's Not Wrong Doesn't Make It Right: From Toddlers to Teens, Teaching Kids to Think and Act Ethically*, by Barbara Coloroso

A favorite documentary film, *Children Full of Life*, pays homage to Toshiro Kanamori, a teacher of 40 ten- and eleven-year-old children in Japan. The film documents a variety of events that happen in one classroom over a single school year. Viewers catch a glimpse of the students' writing and sharing of personal notebook entries. They learn about an art project where students trace each other's bodies on large sheets of paper and complete the shapes with visual images that serve as metaphors of who they are. They watch how the class deals with the boy who loses a parent, how the teacher calms a distraught girl remembering the loss of her grandparent, and how the teacher and his class come to terms with a boy not pulling his weight for a class project that has students ready to sail rafts they have created.

The teacher, Mr. Kanamori, believes that everyone comes to school to learn how to have a happy life and to care for others. For this teacher and his students the class mantra becomes, "If one person is unhappy, we are all unhappy." Mr. Kanamori is kind. Mr. Kanamori is tough. He is determined that for the time he and the students spend together, they will be considerate and caring of one another.

No simple task.

This film, which we share with our teacher candidates, is one way that we help our student teachers discover the importance of creating and maintaining caring classrooms.

Caring: Such a Common-Sense, Basic Thing

We all long for the perfect class—the one where everyone gets along and where there is joy in learning about the curriculum in new and inventive ways. As classroom teachers, we have this longing and so do our students.

Sometimes we get very lucky. The mix of individuals in the class, the circumstances we find ourselves in, the particular physical space, the relationships among class members, and the group dynamics all seem to come together in such a way that the whole experience just "clicks." The classroom is a joy to be in, and there is a hum of activity. A sense of purpose and an overall feeling of respect pervade the room. Experienced teachers recognize when they are having a very good year because everyone in the classroom gets along, trusting the work, trusting each other, trusting themselves.

In other years things don't go as smoothly. There are difficulties in terms of learning and behavioral challenges as well as varying levels of student interest. There does not seem to be enough time to do what needs to be done. The space is too crowded, and the kinds of events and lessons planned seem too difficult.

Many of the factors are hard to pinpoint. Lessons that worked well with other classes seem to fall flat. An uneasiness about the work masks itself as disinterest. There might be an underlying tone of disrespect, of low self-esteem. One or two individuals might set things off. There might be issues connected to chronic bullying and exclusive cliques. Yes, there are moments where everything comes together but, more often than not, the class is disrupted by unhappy events that seem out of teacher control. Everyone feels unsettled. Things are not working.

We cannot spend every summer hoping that next year's perfect class will come along as if by magic. Doing so would make teaching and learning too uneven, too hit and miss, too hard on the soul. There needs to be a way to create a culture of caring about one another, about the work, and about the community both inside and outside the classroom, a culture that is connected to the learning in school and to the future goals of living privately happy and publicly useful lives.

We need to spend time creating a non-competitive culture of listening and cooperation, and an ethic of hearing and valuing everyone's voice. Some teachers might say they don't have time to do this: that it takes too much planning, energy, and time away from the real purpose of education—to teach the curriculum. Our response is that creating this culture *is* the curriculum: that teaching students how to respect one another, value differing opinions, share common experiences, and work towards a critical understanding of complex relationships and ideas is at least partly what school should be about. The goal of any inclusive pedagogy is to create learning environments that reflect, affirm, celebrate, and validate the diversity and complexity of the human experience.

Caring about creating caring classrooms does *not* mean lowering our expectations for ourselves or for our students. It means looking at individual students, groups, and the whole class and making curricular decisions based on what we see and glean from the data we collect. Lisa Delpit reminds us about how important it is to maintain high academic expectations for all students coupled with resources that support high achievement. That is why we need to look critically at what is in place in terms of inclusive curriculum so that we can make the necessary changes in our teaching and learning environments.

Here's a story to support becoming a caring teacher. Chip and Dan Heath, authors of *Switch: How to Change Things When Change Is Hard*, tell a story about a young adolescent who was living life with a "School stinks" mentality. Bobby was described as full of "bad" behaviors—constantly late for school, rarely doing his work, disruptive and threatening. A chaotic home life was outlined as one reason for poor school performance—every school has its Bobbys. School counsellors worked hard to find a solution to give Bobby success.

When asked to identify a time in school when he didn't get into trouble so much, Bobby answered:

BOBBY: I never get in trouble, well, not a lot, in Mrs. Smith's class.
COUNSELLOR: What's different about Mrs. Smith's class?
BOBBY: I don't know, she's nicer. We get a long great.
COUNSELLOR: What exactly does she do that's nicer?

We need to approach the curriculum from a multi-faceted perspective, taking into account content, pedagogy, access, and climate.

Helping to dig deeper into the problem, Bobby explained that Mrs. Smith seemed to help him behave well. Other teachers usually avoided Bobby, but Mrs. Smith always greeted him as soon as he walked into class. She modified the workload, giving different assignments that were explained more fully for him to complete successfully. As others worked in the class, she checked with him to ensure that he understood the instructions, felt connected to the work, and was challenged but not overwhelmed by what was asked of him. The work had to fulfill a purpose for him.

Recognizing the bright spots and moving into action is the stuff of being a better teacher for our students. To give students positive attention seems such a common-sense, basic thing. So simple. So important. This story about Bobby's caring teacher serves as a wakeup to the possibilities of what can happen when we work towards finding and igniting bright spots.

Switch: How to Change Things When Change Is Hard by Chip Heath and Dan Heath (2011) offers narratives and research in psychology and sociology that help shed light on how we can effect transformative change.

The Five *C*s: An Evolving Goal

Creating Caring Classrooms started out to be a book on dealing mainly with bullying issues. We hoped to provide a range of resources, strategies, and frameworks to encourage young people to learn, through literacy and arts events, empathetic understanding through active engagement. We intended to offer teachers a number of text forms and lesson templates that we had developed over the years. With good intentions, we wanted to help teachers prepare their students for times that they might be caught in bullying situations and help them deal with situations where they witnessed hateful behavior. Despite the hundreds of resources in print, online, and through the media that provide guides to teachers and parents to help them deal with the bully, comfort and empathize with the bullied, and empower the bystander, the problem persists. There is no road map for dealing with the bully dilemma.

As we worked together, we realized that the bully issue, although important, is often the outcome of complicated relationships and dynamics that need to be unpacked in various ways. So we decided to address the bigger picture: how teachers could work from the beginning to build on the individual strengths of each student to establish classroom environments of trust and respect.

From our own experience, we knew the benefits of caring classrooms on students' self-esteem, academic motivation, and individual and collective successes. We knew the value of addressing the emotional and spiritual needs of the classroom and the importance of adults treating students with the care and respect that they would extend to their own children.

Our goal is to help teachers tap into the locations, identities, and realities of their students as they share power in the classroom. Our hope is to give teachers ideas about how to nurture student voices as they invest personal interest and increased effort in their own learning.

Creating Caring Classrooms therefore offers a structure for some ideas and strategies for taking control of the classroom agenda so that you and your students can co-create caring classrooms where respect for others is shown, where individual and collective identities are honored, where kindness and concern become crucial backdrops for critical conversations—about the curriculum, about each other, and about the future that lies before us. This book is organized around five *C*s:

Community
Communication
Collaboration
Compassion
Confronting the bully issue

Each of these represents a phase of development.

Confronting bullying is about building healthy relationships. In our classrooms, we need to build a *community* where members can trust, connect with one another, and share.

We need to enrich *communication* skills so students feel comfortable enough to share ideas and prod each other to think, question, explain, guess, predict, wonder, and grow. We need to provide contexts for talk where students share ideas out loud and listen and respond to what is offered by those around them.

Extending communication skills, we feel that it is important to provide opportunities where students engage in *collaboration*. In this way they can learn to solve problems, brainstorm, negotiate, plan, and develop events where everyone can feel success. When learning to collaborate effectively, students can come to appreciate the power of being part of a group of any size. Opportunities for students to work effectively with those having different interests, skills, talents, backgrounds, and identities move students to a better understanding of cooperating and collaborating.

In the next phase in our development scheme, where students have grown as a community, we build *compassion*. As students work together and respond to texts about caring and compassion, they can learn to care and to be compassionate.

Ultimately, the success in each of these phases can lead to *confronting bullying issues*. By stepping into the shoes of others, by dealing with the tough questions, by making connections to personal and world stories, students can reach an understanding of why someone behaves as a bully. They can be prepared to take action when ongoing, deliberate taunting and threats arise. They can come to learn to care.

More Cs for the classroom framework

It is hoped that any of the games, lessons, activities, and tips we provide will help teachers achieve a caring atmosphere, but throughout each school day, attention to consistency needs to be paid.

A caring classroom is like the caring medical clinic whose sign caught our attention. The sign indicated that the clinic is about care, comfort, and confidence. Like that medical clinic, a caring classroom inspires *comfort* and *confidence* within and among all community members. *Cooperation* and *creativity* are other words that could be added to the *C* framework of the book. For this to be achieved, we need to strive for another important *C*: *consistency*.

Language Matters

We also need to pay attention to language and become critically aware of how we speak to our students and to our colleagues. The words that we use in classrooms, labs, hallways, cafeterias, dance studios, gymnasia, and soccer fields can be key mechanisms for both oppression and transformation.

If we spend some time being more conscious of the language we use, we become more mindful of its power. In a book titled *Moral Grandeur and Spiritual Audacity*, Susannah Heschel refers to her famous father, an American rabbi and one of the leading Jewish theologians of the 20th century who marched in the Selma Civil Rights March with Martin Luther King, Jr., in 1965. Heschel comments on the importance that her father placed on words:

> He used to remind us that the Holocaust did not begin with the building of crematoria, and Hitler did not come to power with tanks and guns; it all began with the uttering of evil words, with defamation, with language and propaganda. Words create worlds, he

Moral Grandeur and Spiritual Audacity is a collection of essays by Abraham Heschel, edited by Susannah Heschel (New York: Farrar, Strauss and Giroux, 1996).

Power in What We Say

As a student in the pre-service Teacher Education program at York University, Faculty of Education, Danielle Miller shared this insight:

"I have seen the positive power of the teacher's words countless times. A recent example occurred during my practicum. A not-too-confident student was reading the stage directions of a play in an applied English class. He generally participated in the class with little enthusiasm and never seemed excited about his projects. As he was reading, my mentor teacher [David Wagman] interrupted him and said, 'I am sorry. I'm going to have to stop you right there.' Instantly, I saw the fear in the student's eyes. He was bracing himself for criticism. Instead, my mentor teacher exclaimed: 'Has anyone ever told you what a beautiful voice you have? You should consider a career in radio or news.'

"I watched the boy's face as he went from shock, to realization, and finally to a profound sense of joy. Of course, he did this without smiling, because that wouldn't have been cool. As he read his parts through the rest of the class, he never missed a cue, and the quiet pride he felt was unmistakable in his physicality.

"As a teacher, I will strive to maintain awareness of the wonderful gift that is speech, and use it to spread positive support. It is a tool that can uplift and inspire, but it also can cause terrible damage if used improperly."

used to tell me when I was a child. They must be used very carefully. Some words, once having been uttered, gain eternity and can never be withdrawn. The book of Proverbs reminds us, he wrote, that death and life are in the power of the tongue. (pp. viii–ix)

Being mindful of how we use language in our work matters. Most students enter school expecting that the adults who are entrusted with their care will work on their behalf for their personal and academic success as well as for their present and future happiness. All teachers want the community of students in their classrooms to feel that they are individually as well as collectively valued. Teachers want their classrooms to be places where there is not just tolerance but respect; where there is not just group process but community; where there are not just connections but relationships; and where empathy and compassion are based on understanding rather than on superficial encounters.

We know that we have enormous power to influence the future of the students in our care. We need to be mindful of that power and to remain consistently conscious of what it means to teach fairly in an unfair world. It's essential that we continually "check ourselves," that we self-monitor what we are saying, thinking, feeling, and doing in the classrooms and hallways of our schools. We need to be cognizant of our students' reactions and realities, and know when to change direction if necessary, while approaching learning tasks with sensitivity and discretion.

Seeing ourselves as part of the school community

If we are intent on creating caring classrooms, we must strive to know and understand the communities in which our students live and to recognize how gender, race, ethnicity, immigrant status, social class, urban/rural context, national origin, sexual orientation, and linguistic backgrounds shape interactions in the classroom. We need to stop and gain information so that we are not seen as tourists in the school community but as people who are part of the wider community and who have an interest and a stake in what is happening there and in our classrooms. In efforts to educate ourselves about the rich diversity of the students in our classrooms, we need to promote respect for others, encourage close personal relationships, structure effective communication contexts, and imbue in everyone an engaged concern for the common good.

The following observations on community come from Jacqueline Spence, who serves as central coordinating principal, equity & inclusive schools, Student, Parent and Community School Services, Toronto District School Board.

Walking the Talk of Community Engagement

As an administrator in an inner-city school, I learned many things, with the importance of building trusting relationships with parents and members of the wider community topping the list. I realized that if I truly wanted to create a school community where all students were performing to the best of their ability, I had to understand their daily lived experience. So, I had to be visible not only within the school but also in the community.

I remember one day following a student home because I knew that this student lived next door to a student who had been absent for many days. I had tried to reach the parents by phone but was unsuccessful, so I decided to do a home visit. A parent from the school asked me what I was doing walking through the neighborhood—"Principals don't do that here." At that moment, I understood that as educators, particularly in inner-city communities, we must "walk" the talk of community engagement.

In working with teacher candidates in the Urban Diversity Program at York University, I had the unique opportunity to contribute to a teacher preparation program that put the importance of community at the forefront. Given that the schools where teacher candidates are placed are in inner-city communities, an understanding of the connection of community to school system is essential, as most of the teacher candidates and teachers within the school do not live in the community. At the beginning of each of my three years in the program, there were always students who did not understand the connection between community and school. They insisted that working in the community was not "teaching," and they wanted to learn how to teach. On some level, I agreed with this statement. Most of the time, the teacher candidates were not *teaching* in their community placements—they were *learning*. By requiring students to do a community placement for a minimum of 40 hours as a part of their course work, the importance of community was emphasized in a meaningful way. The work that the teacher candidates engaged in ranged from helping to plan a Good Food Market to supporting a film-making program run by social workers. Their placement allowed teacher candidates to work with students outside of the traditional classroom setting and gain some insight into the daily lived experiences of the students.

Creating Caring Classrooms Throughout the Year

The Decisive Element

Consider these words of Haim Ginatt and how they might apply to us:

"I have come to a frightening conclusion. I am the decisive element in the classroom. It is my personal approach that creates the climate. It is my daily mood that makes the weather. As a teacher, I possess tremendous power to make a child's life joyous. I can be a tool for torture or an instrument of inspiration. I can humiliate or humour; hurt or heal. In all situations it is my response that decides whether a crisis will be escalated or de-escalated, a child humanized or de-humanized."

This book is about helping students gain personal power, establish rewarding relationships, and find fulfilling work in school. It takes time to look after these things in the classroom. One thing that we are advocating is taking the time to do this kind of work—to listen to each other, talk through problems, find out others' opinions as they talk themselves into understanding, telling personal stories connected to the activities. When it comes to time, doing the kinds of activities outlined in this book definitely represents a challenge. Our advice is to find ways of weaving these activities into what you are already doing in your classroom.

The first days of the school year are often about establishing class expectations, outlining routines, doing getting-to-know-each-other activities, and building a trustful relationship between teacher and students, and the students who will be sitting alongside each other from day to day.

There is usually some attempt to build community.

But what happens in the classroom beyond the first day of school? What events help to enrich a sense of community? How will students continue to find the space between the four walls a zone of safety? How will students come to understand and work with those who are similar or different in needs and interests? How will our students work alone, in pairs, in small groups, or as a whole class to work and learn together: to laugh, to create, and to be comfortable enough—safe enough—to share ideas, stories, and feelings with anyone and everyone?

Our advice is to build community not only at the beginning of the year but all through it and not as a separate event but woven into curriculum events. Looking after the learning community becomes part of the everyday work in the classroom, and as time goes by, barriers between students come down, and wonderful friendships and relationships are built.

We encourage novice and experienced teachers to choose the activities and ideas that will work for your particular class. Feel free to amend, adapt, and extend the activities in new ways. Don't be surprised to find that your students respond in unanticipated ways that take the work in a new direction. Probably the best thing to do is to go along with what they are offering up and be surprised by their innovative ideas, by the connections being established among them, and by the new, strong, and respectful relationships that emerge. We hope that you will use this resource to facilitate the students' journeys of personal discovery and empathetic response to each other, to their community, and to other individuals and groups they meet along the way.

Key Chapter Components

The five chapters have a number of features in common, including, of course, an introduction and teaching tips. Depending on chapter theme, however, the balance between the various components will differ. For example, many games promote community building.

- Introductory text sets the context and establishes the skill and content focus for the chapter. Each chapter begins with a pertinent focus quotation.
- Games and activities provide many ways to develop aspects of a caring classroom. Specifically, they offer a foundation and mental set for working well to build community, communication, and collaboration, the first three phases of creating a caring classroom.
- Lessons, sometimes referred to as events, are comprised of instructions that integrate literacy strategies and artistic endeavours. These connect to curriculum expectations, as well as to guidelines that support the creative process and critical thinking.
- Teaching tips offer suggestions for classroom management and for working in group situations, as well as considerations for meeting the instructional needs for a diversity of learners. They always appear as boxed text.
- Literature resources reinforce chapter themes. Fiction and non-fiction sources for exploration include picture books, novel excerpts, scripts, visual images, poetry, and newspaper articles.
- Beyond the use of literature in specific lessons, there are recommended resources: both up-to-date lists of children's literature that you can draw on to support students' learning and reference material that can be used to enrich programming and instruction.
- Reflection and assessment are addressed through key questions and prompts. The book encompasses teacher, group, and self-assessment. Some tools appear as line masters.
- As a special book feature, there are Spotlights on the Classroom, articles in which guest contributors describe authentic classroom experiences and provide practical suggestions for implementing lessons.

Caring Teachers: What Students Say

The students in Rachael Stein's Grade 6 class were challenged to write letters to beginning teachers enrolled in an Initial Teacher Education program. Putting their thoughts to paper, the students were able to reflect on how the classroom as a whole could be a caring place. The students offer advice to any teacher concerned about making the classroom a community.

Have trust in your students and faith that they will try their best in every subject and every class. (A.T.)

If you want to be a caring teacher, you must respect the students and other teachers working at the school. You must come to your work happy to teach. (R.K.)

Here is my idea for being an awesome, caring teacher. You will have to be respectful to your students. Respect them with your whole heart. (D.L.)

Don't worry if your students won't listen to you at first. You make them be the best students and they will make you be the best teacher. (T.R.)

It's a bit harder than you think. Not only do you have to teach and make sure everyone is listening. You have to pay attention to your students. (J.B.)

You have to be kind to others and make smiles. (A.P.)

I think that to be a caring teacher you have to get to really know your students. Get to know the things they like and what they don't like. Find out what they like to do in school and when you find out about them, it will help you make fun lessons and show the students that you care about their interests and how they learn. They will be glad that you care about them, and they will enjoy being in your class. Good luck! (S.P.)

A teacher can be caring by putting fun in the lessons and understanding that if you are having fun, they are likely also having fun. (T.L.)

Chapter 1

Building Community

Community provides a unifying force, it increases commitment among students and teachers; it lessens alienation and improves motivation; it gives teachers greater autonomy and harnesses the human potential that is in every social situation; and it gives students a greater stake in a school and increases their identification with it. Without community school is just a place to get through as painlessly as possible; with community, it is our school, a place in which to live and find meaning.

—From *High Schools as Communities: The Small School Reconsidered* by T. B. Gregory and G. R. Smith (p. 57)

Community is a word heard a lot in educational circles. In this particular case we are talking about the learning community that exists in the classroom in relationship to other classes, the school as a whole, and the community beyond the classroom.

It is important that everyone feels that they are part of the classroom experience, that they are included, honored, and valid community members who won't be judged for who they are and how they present themselves in the classroom. One thing that we have found over the years is to spend time getting to know one another—finding out each other's names, learning about where everyone comes from, having a chance to actively engage with one another so that there is laughter, involvement, and activity. You will find that a change comes over the room and that solidarity among all class members is established as you do these activities. You are making memories as you talk, laugh, move, and engage with one another. You are creating a community of learners who can support one another through good times and bad.

We know that in order for students to find their confidence as learners, they need to have an empathetic teacher—one who understands their particular learning needs, intelligences, and gifts. Students shine when the teacher proposes that they do things that have a certain degree of challenge to them—a pleasurable intensity—but that connect to the students' interests and backgrounds. These activities are ways for students to challenge themselves to excel. We also know that students will achieve if they feel that they belong: that they are understood for who they are at this point in their history. That's what these activities do: they provide a way for students to get to know one another as individuals and gain a collective identity.

Among other variables, the claim could be made that the most effective classroom is one with a caring, positive, and cooperative learning environment. We know that students bring unique experiences, backgrounds, personalities, and needs inside the walls of a classroom. Teachers are challenged to become conductors of the multi-faceted chorus, guiding the development of a harmonic symphony that melds individual abilities and circumstances together. Students need to feel free to investigate, take risks, and learn. When students and teachers work together to cultivate a learning environment where a sense of trust is created, school can be a place for developing social attachments and valuing the well-being of peers. In this way, the classroom can be a community, a place of belonging.

Doing the Groundwork

The following 20 practices represent some important ways for teachers to establish a groundwork for creating a classroom as a community.

1. Write end-of-summer letters to families.

For students who have lost their way or who feel that they are not good in school, this letter can be a ticket of hope. It is a really positive, empowering way to begin the school year even before you have met your students!

Send a letter home to each member of the new class, introducing yourself and telling children how much you are looking forward to meeting them and having them in your class. Tell a bit about yourself, how you spent your summer, and what you like about teaching. You might ask a few questions that you genuinely want the answers to. Reassure students by reminding them that everyone will probably be feeling a little nervous on the first day. Be enthusiastic. This letter is an opportunity for you to connect individually with each student and family and to plant optimism and respect in the minds of your students. This year is a new beginning and promises to be the best ever!

2. Prepare a welcoming environment.

Before classes start, take a good long look at the classroom that you have been assigned. If you had the room last year, pitch out old work from former students and throw out the old so you can bring in the new. Think about real-estate agents who encourage clients to get rid of clutter so that potential buyers can "see" themselves in the house or apartment they are thinking of buying. It is the same with students. Let them enter the space and see it as a place where they can make their mark (literally and figuratively). Find ways of making the classroom space welcoming, not overwhelming. Try to limit your imprint. Organize the space, but restrain yourself from decorating it. The decoration will happen throughout the year as students' writing, photos, messages, and projects fill up the space. The classroom then becomes a collaborative space that belongs to the students who inhabit it.

3. Create a space that works.

You also need to face the space and decide how to set up the room so that students have time to work independently as well as collaboratively. You could begin the first day with independent desks but gradually change configurations as you get to know your students better. There will be times when everyone might need to sit in a circle; other times they need to work independently.

How you get students to move into groups effortlessly and with minimal noise needs to be worked out as well. The classroom should have a flow about it—and moving lots of bodies around for maximum learning needs to be figured out so that the thought of it does not overwhelm you. As students learn they will be expected to work in many different configurations—alone, with various partners, in small groups, as a large class—they will help you decide how to do it quickly and efficiently. They don't want to waste time either, especially if there is something interesting to learn!

4. Greet the students by name.

On the first day of school, stand outside the classroom and welcome every student into the class by name. If you don't know a student's name, ask the student to tell it to you and get advice about spelling and pronunciation. This is a wonderful way for you to take attendance and make a personal connection with each student. You won't have to take attendance once the bell has rung. No one has to be embarrassed or singled out. Instead, you can plan for a more interesting, creative beginning to the school year.

Of course, greeting the students should go beyond the first day. Welcoming the students into the classroom, a simple question or statement will do, for example: "How was your weekend?" "How was your hockey game last night?" "How's your dog?" "I like your shoes."

5. Connect with the parents.

Make sure that you connect to the parents waiting outside the classroom—not just the ones whom you know. If the parents do not speak English, find a way of communicating with them and letting them know that you are very happy to meet them and that you hope that there will be many times to meet about their child's progress throughout the year. Make everyone feel welcome. Remember: this is the opening act and all eyes are on you.

6. Set class rules and routines.

Sometime during the first days, you will need to establish some rules and routines with the class. The best thing to do is to ask for suggestions: "What should a caring classroom look like? What should a learning classroom look like? What should an inclusive classroom look like?" Don't hesitate to tell your students why this kind of learning environment is important to establish. Share your philosophy with them. They might not appear that interested, but they really are. They want to have a positive year and if they feel that they have a stake in how the classroom dynamics will be established, there will be much more "buy in." If some students are too shy to speak out loud, have them fill in a small form with their suggestions. They don't have to sign their name—but make sure you tell them that you welcome their ideas.

7. Plan together.

Filling the Space

When the students in Brian Crawford's Grade 4/5 class came to school on the first day, they noticed that all the furniture and equipment had been removed from the room. On the first morning, the children worked in groups to design their classroom home.

It is important to have students think about the kind of classroom they want to call home for the next year. Ask them to make suggestions about how to "operationalize" their ideas.

- What will our caring classroom look like? feel like? sound like?
- What can we do on our own and together to make sure that our goals are met?
- What should we refrain from doing?
- What should we do if we run into problems?
- How will we know whether we have achieved our goals?

8. Agree on positive classroom symbols.

Have students brainstorm symbols that might help them visualize a caring classroom (e.g., dove and olive branch, hearts, a handshake, a hand extended). Brainstorm words that could be synonymous with caring. Research words and symbols in other languages and cultures that represent caring. Create a mural or a poster that can be hung on the wall or door of the classroom. Make sure that everyone contributes to the mural and that all names are recorded.

9. Go, Team, Go!

Come up with a class name that everyone likes, for example, the Fortunate Fours, the Fab Fives, the Stellar Sixes, the Suave Sevens, the Crazy Eights.

10. Determine how to begin and end.

If you are in a school where your classes move from one room to the next, the challenge is to find ways of making the home space welcoming in other ways. Try negotiating this with your students by asking the following questions: "How can we begin each class together? What routines can we all do that will make the class feel more like a community? What should we do before we all depart the space? What rules need to be set so that the room is rearranged for the next class to enter? How can we all share that responsibility?"

11. Establish a forum.

Establish a space where everyone meets to share ideas. Meeting on a class carpet is an important ritual for students to plan, discuss, reflect, sing songs, listen to stories, and meet to discuss relevant issues. Hold a class meeting early in the first week to make sure that students understand that their ideas matter, that all voices are important, that bullying and exclusion will not be tolerated. You might give students an overview of the year—what kinds of things they will be learning, the class excursions, the guests who will be invited in, the performances they will attend, the major curriculum themes and big ideas that will be explored. Consider this the time to "pitch" the kind of year you are envisioning for them and to get their input and reactions. They need to see the year ahead as purposeful, engaging, exciting, and inclusive of all of them.

12. Hold class meetings.

Continue having class meetings during the year. Class meetings do not have to be long, but they do have to be held at regular intervals. They should always have a specific purpose and a way of ensuring that all voices are heard. Consider having rotating chairpersons so that everyone understands and experiences what it is like to run a meeting. You will have to teach students how to do this. If some students lack the confidence, have them run a small committee meeting first. The meetings can focus on more than problem solving, voting on issues, discussing concerns, or planning special trips or events. Students could brainstorm a list of topics that they feel need to be addressed in their lives: school uniforms, cell phone use in schools, and environmental issues in and around the school. Meetings can also be called when special guests are in the school. People can be invited to meetings to sit on panels where the class asks questions. In all sorts of ways, students grow into a community of learners where they are encouraged to be active and to participate.

13. Involve the students in communication with families.

Parent open houses do not have to be organized just by you. You could have the class determine what work has been significant at the various intervals during the year. Ask them: "What needs to be highlighted? How can we best represent what we have learned?" Make sure that everyone shines in some way—that no one is left out. You might have students work in small committees reflecting on what has been accomplished during the first few weeks of school.

Have the class decide how to present this learning to their parents and guardians. There could be video snippets, a group performance, or perhaps an audio-visual presentation. Encourage students to create small-group activities, inviting parents to become involved in kinds of learning that have been taking place. Invite students to consider, "What did you do that your parents would find fascinating to participate in?" This is a wonderful chance to reinforce learning, presentation skills, and the feeling that the class is truly the students'.

14. Engage in outreach.

When is a good time to reach out to other classes in the school or to the community that lies beyond the school? You might decide to work with a younger class, meet the students at the local high school, or establish an ongoing relationship with some senior citizens in a local senior citizens home. Again, the work needs to be negotiated, have a purpose, and be challenging and worthwhile. It is important that students be required to exert a fair amount of effort.

15. Encourage leadership.

One purpose of a caring classroom is to help students hone their leadership skills. For everyone to benefit, encourage collaborative leadership, where students take on different roles and responsibilities at different times in groups so that they learn new skills. Some students might need to learn how to listen, others how to encourage, others to initiate, and others to cooperate. The teaching of group process skills is paramount in establishing a classroom that works.

16. Reward group accomplishment.

Consider rethinking extrinsic rewards for some and not all. Some classroom communities get completely shut down by the rewarding of food (e.g., pizza lunches) to those students who were successful and by the withdrawal of prizes to those students who failed to accomplish what was asked of them. You need to let your students know that the prize is the work—the feeling that comes from group accomplishment—and that no food, money, or other prizes will be awarded by you for the work done.

If the whole class decides that they need a reward, however, that is an entirely different thing. When this happens, the reward comes from within—and the classroom will be a far happier place. Celebrate small successes throughout the year. Honor all efforts. Include everyone, everyone, everyone.

If you are planning a celebration of some kind, remember that this event needs to be inclusive of all the people in the class. Invitations might have to be written in many languages; times might have to be negotiated to get as many family members at the event as possible.

17. Promote high expectations.

Part of a caring classroom is caring about the quality of the work and setting high expectations for everyone. There is some truth to the idea that "caring is believing" and that students can achieve what is expected of them. It is also true that high curriculum expectations have to be matched with the right amount of support, understanding, time, approaches, and resources. So, get to know your students and help them understand what they are learning, how they will benefit from this knowledge, when they will recognize personal successes and learning achievement. Challenge them to see themselves as lifelong learners.

18. Help students play together.

To learn how to work together, students also need to know how to play together. There are a range of verbal and non-verbal, physical and non-physical games that promote social–emotional growth as well as promoting skills of communication and collaboration, cooperation and competition. (The beginnings of Chapters 1, 2, and 3 of this book offer a variety of games that encourage students to join in together, to create together, and to have fun together.)

19. Troubled water: Build a bridge.

What's the plan if you run into some rough water—if communication breaks down and people begin to not work together? This is bound to happen—communication breakdown is part of all ongoing human interaction. Hurt feelings and misunderstandings are to be expected and need to be talked through. Conflict resolution strategies are essential to know in the caring classroom. Make sure that you have a plan. In this book you will discover some meaningful routines to put in place for students to discuss problems and conflicts.

20. Foster independence.

The ultimate aim of the caring classroom is to guide students to independence. Through the teacher gradually releasing responsibility, students see themselves as learners who can identify for themselves and for group members the kinds of actions they need to undertake to be successful in school and to lead happy and useful lives in the future. Assessment *for* learning, *as* learning, and *of* learning needs to be entwined in the work so that students can assess their long-term and short-term goals. They need to learn how to self-monitor their capacity to communicate effectively as members of the classroom community while working in partners, in small groups, and with the whole class. They will grow to understand that their purpose is to learn by collaborating and supporting others as they engage with activities that are relevant, imaginative, challenging, and open-ended.

Events That Build Classroom Community

What are some classroom events you have introduced to build community in your own classroom? Have you considered the following? Which of these events have you tried? Which might you try?

- ☐ Class trip
- ☐ Daily Read-Aloud
- ☐ Sharing of personal stories
- ☐ Class newsletter
- ☐ Celebration of the learning with others
- ☐ Science fair
- ☐ Play presentation
- ☐ Preparation for an assembly
- ☐ Publishing of student work
- ☐ Creation of a mural
- ☐ Buddying with another class
- ☐ Classroom helpers
- ☐ Creation of bulletin-board displays
- ☐ Inquiry projects
- ☐ Pen pals
- ☐ "Where are you from?" maps
- ☐ Class quilt
- ☐ Fundraising project
- ☐ Singing together
- ☐ Poetry anthology
- ☐ Creation of a cooperative book
- ☐ Potluck
- ☐ Hot topics drawn from news events
- ☐ SMART Board activity
- ☐ Class meeting
- ☐ Greet 'em at the door!
- ☐ Board Game Day
- ☐ Special days (e.g., Funky Hair Day, Hat Day)
- ☐ Artist in the classroom
- ☐ Talent show
- ☐ Choral speaking
- ☐ Shared reading
- ☐ Birthday celebrations!
- ☐ Student of the Week
- ☐ Extracurricular clubs
- ☐ Class mission statement
- ☐ School or class T-shirts
- ☐ Baking
- ☐ Being an audience for a film, play, or concert
- ☐ Snack days
- ☐ Art show/Art gallery

Games That Build Community

Each of the following games serves to build a sense of inclusion among students.

Let's Start with Our Names

Students stand in a circle. In turn, they introduce themselves to the group by calling out their names. The activity is repeated. This time the students each add a simple gesture (e.g., a wave of hand or a finger snap) as they call out their names. The name and gesture are passed around the circle so that each person has a chance to repeat everyone's name. One person can be chosen to lead the game, and the gesture can be passed to the right. Everyone gets a chance to be a "leader."

Variation #1: Students call out their names with an accompanying gesture. The whole group echoes the name and gesture.

Variation #2: The game is repeated with students creating a new gesture that hasn't been used. Players can be encouraged to use their voices in different ways (e.g., shouting, whispering, or singing).

Rhythmic Names

With thanks to Bob Barton

1. Students are arranged in a circle and introduce themselves by their first names.
2. A finger-snapping rhythm is established. Students introduce themselves by saying "My name is …" and as appropriate, the group answers: "His name is …" "Her name is …"

AHMED: My name is Ahmed.
GROUP: His name is Ahmed.
ZOE: My name is Zoe.
GROUP: Her name is Zoe.

3. The activity is repeated, still with a finger-snapping rhythm being established. This time, however, students introduce themselves by saying their first name and sharing one statement about themselves (a fact, an interest or hobby, a feeling). The group echoes what each person says.

AHMED: My name is Ahmed and I have a goldfish.
GROUP: His name is Ahmed and he has a goldfish.
ZOE: My name is Zoe and I go skating.
GROUP: Her name is Zoe and she goes skating.

Variation #1: Students each say both first name and last name.

Variation #2: Change the finger-snapping rhythm, perhaps by adding a clap. Students can all have the same topic to share, for example, "My favorite food is …," "I read …," or "I've travelled to …"

Variation #3: At the conclusion of any activity, each student can share one thing that he or she learned about someone in the group.

Name Stories

With thanks to Belarie Zatzman

Everyone has a name. Behind every name is a story. To begin students can turn to one or two friends to tell a story about their name. The following questions can be used to guide the discussion:

- What does their name mean?
- Why did their parents choose to give them this name?
- Were they named after someone?
- Do they have a nickname?
- Do they like their name?
- Do they know their name in another language?
- If they had a chance to choose another name, what would that be? Why?
- Do they have more than one name? If so, are they willing to share their other given names with the class?

To enrich community building, students can each be given an opportunity to share a story about their name. Students can discuss any commonalities in the stories. What were some surprises they encountered in any of the shared stories? What do these stories tell them about their diversity? This activity is significant in helping students recognize diversity among the group.

Extensions

1. Some students can find out more information about what their names mean by using the Internet or by asking family members questions.
2. Students may wish to write these name stories to share with others. Have the students add a picture or a name crest. These name stories could be collated into a book called "Our Name Stories" which students take home to share with their families.

Getting to Know You

Ask the students to print their names in the centre of a piece of paper. In the top right-hand corner, students list one quality which they like about themselves. In the top left-hand corner, students list one accomplishment of which they are proud. In the bottom left-hand corner, students list one thing that is their favorite (e.g., color, food, or animal). In the bottom right-hand corner, students list one possession that is special to them.

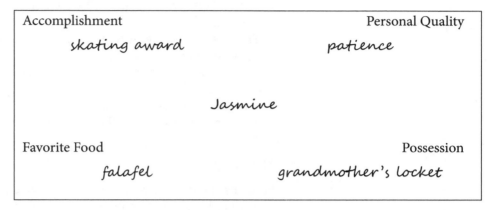

Students now pin the papers to their chests or hold the paper in front them and circulate around the room, following teacher directions.

1. To begin, the students conduct the activity without talking, reading as many profiles as they can in the allotted time.
2. On a signal, students are told that they can talk with any people they meet about the listed items. The activity continues for several minutes so that students can interact with more than one player.
3. Students work in pairs and have conversations prompted by the items that have been listed on the sheets. Students might wish to ask questions to find out more about their partner's background.
4. Students work in groups of six or eight. Students take turns to introduce partners to the rest of the group.

"I've Got Mail"

Students sit in an open circle with no empty chairs. A volunteer stands in the middle. The goal is to have the person in the middle find a place in the circle. That person says, "I've got mail for …" and finishes the statement (e.g., "for everyone wearing glasses"). Everyone who is wearing glasses rises and runs to sit down in a different seat. Those who do not have glasses remain seated. Players cannot go back to the same chair in the same round. The person left standing without a chair is now in the middle and calls out a different "I've got mail …" statement (e.g., for everyone who lives in an apartment, for everyone who ate cookies this week, for everyone who has a birthday in the summer).

"The Seat on My Right Is Free"

Establish the rule that everyone should receive an invitation and that no person can be invited more than once.

Students sit on chairs in a circle in which one chair is empty. The person to the left of the chair says: "The seat on my right is free. I would like to invite [someone in the class] to sit beside me." The person who is invited crosses the circle, which frees up a chair beside somebody else. The game continues as the person to the left of the empty chair repeats: "The seat on my right is free. I would like [name of classmate] to sit beside me."

Extension
Working with different language registers and commands can help students, especially English Language Learners, to express themselves:

- The seat on my left is free … I would be so happy if Perlina came and sat beside me.
- The seat on my right is free … Daniel, would you be so kind as to come and sit beside me?
- The seat on my left is free … Saadia, please come here right now and sit beside me!
- The seat on my right is free … Raymond, it would be such a pleasure if you would consider crossing the circle to sit beside me.

String Toss

Students stand in a circle. One player is given a ball of string (or yarn) and that player holds the end but tosses the ball of string to any group member. The first player asks, "What was something you read this week?" After the second player answers, she or he tosses the ball to another group member, while holding onto a piece of string and asks the person receiving the ball a new question. Eventually, the circle should look like a web, signifying how the group is connected.

Extension
Students can be encouraged to make statements about themselves, such as "I am a middle child." A person in the circle who wants to connect to that statement in some way puts up a hand to have the yarn tossed his or her way. Then the player says: "I am a middle child too. I have an older brother and a younger sister." Someone who relates to the second statement then puts up a hand and adds another dimension to the unfolding story by saying, "I have a half-brother and a step-sister." The game continues until the yarn has been sent to everyone in the circle.

A Hen, a Pen

Once students catch on to this game, it tends to be a favorite.

Students sit in a large circle. One person, perhaps the teacher, is player 1. This role demands some concentration, and the person playing this part is responsible for keeping the game going. Player 1 turns to the person on the right and recites a line of text. The following script best demonstrates how the game is played:

PLAYER 1 (to player 2): I give you a hen.
PLAYER 2 (to player 1): A what?
PLAYER 1 (to player 2): A hen.
PLAYER 2 (to player 3): This is a hen.
PLAYER 3 (to player 2): A what?
PLAYER 2 (to player 1): A what?
PLAYER 1 (to player 2): A hen.
PLAYER 2 (to player 3): A hen.
PLAYER 3 (to player 4): This is a hen.

Once the game is under way, player 1 turns to the player on the left and says, "I give you a pen." The pen segment is relayed simultaneously with the hen. At one point, a player will receive both the hen and the pen—the trick is to pass both on, in either direction. To make the game work smoothly, players sometimes pass an object in either direction as they say their lines. This may simplify the game—or perhaps cause more confusion!

"I Am a Tree"

Students are organized in groups of five or six. One person is chosen to create a still image of a tree and recites the line "I am a tree." Any group member can choose to enter the scene, adding on to the tree image in some way (e.g., a branch). That person recites the line "I am a branch." A third person adds on to the scene (e.g., a nest) and recites the line "I am a nest." The tree then decides whether to keep the branch or the nest. If chosen, that person remains frozen in the scene. The tree and the one not chosen return to the group, and the activity is repeated.

The rules of this game are to create a still image using three members. The one in the scene from the beginning is the leader and makes a choice about who to keep. As group members watch and decide how to enter, they are encouraged to do so spontaneously and move the game along quickly. The game continues for up to 10 minutes. At the conclusion, students can share some of the unique items they pretended to be.

Variation #1: The game is played sequentially in a circle. Player 1 makes an image quickly followed by player 2 and player 3 who complete the scene. Player 4 creates a completely new image, followed by players 5 and 6. Each player should recite the line "I am a _____."

Variation #2: The game is played with the whole class standing in a circle. One player volunteers to go into the middle to create an image. Anyone from the circle can decide to enter the scene. The game continues until a tableau of five people is created.

Novel Connections
You can use game variation #3 as a way of identifying what students are connecting to in the novel or short story. They can take a look at the tableau that they have created and then write from the perspective of that object or character.

Variation #3: One student enters the circle and assumes a pose and says: "I am the main character of the novel that we are reading. My name is _____." The next person goes in, assumes a pose in direct relation to that character, and identifies who he or she is. Students can be other characters in the novel or can be objects. The game continues until all ideas and characters are exhausted.

Considering Competition

by David Stocker

David Stocker teaches at City View, a Toronto public alternative school devoted to promoting student activism for students in Grades 7 and 8. David is the author of Maththatmatters: A Teacher Resource Linking Math and Social Justice. *He lives with his partner Kathy, who is unschooling their three children, Jazz, Kio, and Storm.*

Imagine this.

Your doctor is standing before you, asking you to choose between taking a red pill and a blue pill. Concerned with due diligence, you ask what the difference is.

"Well, the red pill causes higher levels of anxiety," she begins. "It's also linked to higher levels of depression, leads to more injuries, and those injuries tend to be more serious."

The quizzical look on your face doesn't slow her down. "In studies between those taking the red pill and the blue pill, those taking the red tend to show lower levels of empathy."

The Healthy Red Pill?

The doctor has now registered the concern on your face. "Of course, since the red pill is so popular with people, it's undergone a re-branding campaign to protect its image, and we now refer to it as the *healthy* red pill. We tell people to take less of it, or approach it with a better attitude."

You wonder if that's a little bit like approaching mercury poisoning with a better attitude, but manage to ask instead if, notwithstanding the disadvantages, there are certain benefits to the red pill that cannot be delivered by the blue.

"Let's see," she says, scanning the labels. "Well, there is one thing. The blue pill doesn't leave you with the feeling of joy associated with trouncing someone."

The blank stare on your face prompts her to try again. "You know, crushing someone. Triumphing over them. Putting them in their place. Showing them that you're better than they are. The feelings associated with those things."

"Oh," you say grimly. "Nothing else?"

"Well, many people believe that the red pill causes higher achievement levels," says the doctor with a confident smile.

"Many people *believe* that it does?" you say with an eyebrow raised.

"Well," she hesitates, "research has shown that higher levels of achievement and creativity seem to require the *complete absence* of the red pill. *Notwithstanding* people's beliefs, the higher levels of anxiety and the focus the red pill creates on 'winning' seem to get in the way of 'excellence.' "

"I'll take the blue," you whisper.

"I thought you might," she whispers back.

A Gap Between Research and Practice

Frankly, I'm confused at the education system's love affair with competition (the red pill). For decades, research has consistently condemned mutually exclusive goal attainment— where the success of one person or group depends on another's failure—and called into question the notion that competition in any form would be considered healthy. And yet, in our schools, intramurals and tournaments are pervasive, and the use of marks and grades are as entrenched as ever. When Alfie Kohn published his book *No Contest: The Case Against Competition* and summarized for us the dozens of comparative studies looking at competition and cooperation (the blue pill), I thought, naively, that we could now all link research with practice and come up with some healthy alternatives.

Quiet Protest

And there are many. Fifteen years ago at the small alternative school where I work, I decided to start small. I put away the megaphone that I used to update the game score every 30 seconds and then stopped announcing the score at all. Students who came up to me after the games wanting the final tally were met with "I can't remember, but it looked like fun."

Then I began taking traditional games, such as soccer, volleyball, and basketball, and mucking with the rules in a way that made keeping score impossible to do, or nonsensical.

Almost Soccer is played with at least four teams and pylons are used on each side of a regular playing field to make the nets. Each of the four goalies tailors the net length to their ability and desire for challenge. The goal of the game is to score on any goalie other than your own. Play is continuous and there are at least six soccer balls on the field at a time. Additional challenges and rules are negotiable, and can apply to individuals or the group as a whole.

By the time our third game of Almost Soccer had rolled around, I had one goalie choosing to wear flippers ("I need a bigger challenge, David"), three students sprinting a length of the field after scoring and before returning to play ("Better cardio, you understand"), and several groups of three tying their ankles together to roam four legged after the soccer balls ("We just need to have exclusive access to a few special balls if you're attached to someone"). It wasn't until I looked closely at a string of seven players all attached at the ankles and laughing their way towards a goalie that I realized several in the line-up came from different teams.

Realize that, in Almost Soccer, the only limit to the amount of challenge is your imagination. At least six times as many players are involved in direct play with the ball at any given moment, and it is impossible to keep score in any way. How, indeed, would scoring on a 2 m wide net count as compared to a net somewhat larger or somewhat smaller? With continuous play, it is impossible to keep track of all goals scored for and against other teams. From the usual roster of reasons for enjoying competition, the only one that isn't possible to satisfy in this particular game is the pleasure of beating someone.

An Ongoing Challenge

There's no reason to play traditional games at all, really. When an online search for "cooperative games" can turn up more than four million "hits," the biggest challenge is to find the games that best fit your students' ages and abilities.

I like the game Bump and Scoot, where two "teams" face each other on the volleyball court. Whenever a player successfully volleys the ball over the net, he or she switches sides by scooting under the net during play. Several players may conceivably switch sides during a single play, but each player is allowed to switch only once. The game ends when every single player has switched sides. What this means is that there is only *one* team on the court, *all* of the players working towards a common goal. There is success only if everybody is supported.

For educators who care deeply about the five Cs discussed in this book, consider that it's not the way in which competition is conducted or facilitated, but rather the structure of the interaction itself: that the creation of winners and losers undermines what we value as educators.

It's past time to challenge the sacred cow that competition can ever be healthy.

Story Events That Enrich the Classroom Community

The events, or lessons, that follow are designed to have students create stories and share stories from their lives. They also invite students to consider their interests, strengths, and identities and to communicate these qualities in a group where members are working together to build a sense of trust that can be strengthened only through respectful communication.

Circle Stories

The students are organized into groups of six to eight and sit in a circle. The challenge is for each group to create a story with each person, in turn, contributing a sentence to the story. A time limit could be established for the storytelling to continue.

The following statements are possible beginnings for the storytelling session:

- It was a dark and stormy night.
- It all began in the year 2050.
- Long ago, in a kingdom far away …
- Once on the shores of a sea, a strange box was discovered …
- He was warned to stay away from the cupboard, but one day …
- With the rub of a lamp, the genie was at last released ...
- They all laughed at the idea of a time machine …
- From the outside, you would not know that anyone lived in the house …
- She listened at the door and could hear them whispering about her …
- They had promised him that they would not tell his parents, but ...
- "Have you ever been in trouble with the law before?" the police woman asked.

Variation #1: The above activity is repeated. This time each player contributes only one word to the story.

Variation #2: As each person tells a part of the story, the rest of the group acts out the story in mime. Each student, in turn, can have a chance to add a part of the story; however, for this variation, only the person on the right of the storyteller acts out the story as it is told.

Variation #3: This storytelling activity could be repeated by retelling a tale that the students are familiar with or by working with a story that has just been read aloud to them.

Words of Strength

This game can be played with a package of sticky notes. Tell the students to choose any number of sheets. Some may choose to take one or two; others may choose several.

Once everyone has something to write on, direct them to record a descriptive word on each piece of paper. The adjectives should be positive ones that they think others would use to describe them. If someone has one sheet of paper, that person need only write one adjective (e.g., *kind*). If someone selected five sheets, that person needs to write five adjectives (e.g., *kind, thoughtful, patient, determined, athletic*).

Once students have completed writing, they can work in small groups to share their choices and give reasons why they chose those words. Students can discuss the following:

- What words did players have in common with others in the group?
- What word(s) was the most "surprising"?
- How did you feel writing positive adjectives to describe yourself?

Variation: Instead of adjectives, students write about their lives, saying, for example, "I have two brothers, I have never been on a boat, and I won a prize in the science fair."

Strength Bombardment

Ask students to form groups of five sitting on chairs. Have them number themselves off 1-2-3-4-5. Each student is given a file card. There is to be no talking. The students should focus on each member of their group. Have them write down two things they like about each member of the group. (For example: "Bryan has a good sense of humor and always shares his lunch.") Encourage students to write only positive things that identify each person's strengths. Have students hand in the cards with their own names. Add comments of your own to each card.

The next day, have students retrieve their cards, get into groups, and number themselves off 1-2-3-4-5. On a signal have the students focus their attention on group member 1. They should tell their classmate all of the things that they wrote down about her and add the teacher's comments as well. The goal is to create a "Strength Bombardment." When they have finished, have the students focus on the next person. Everyone should get many compliments—both teacher and student generated. At the end of the exercise debrief about how the exercise made students feel individually and as a group.

In their groups have students answer the following questions:

- How does it make you feel when you get a compliment from your peers?
- How does this exercise help build trust among group members?
- What positive comments from your peers surprised you?
- What did you like about this exercise?
- What did you worry about?
- What would you change about the exercise?

I've Got a Secret!

It works best if all students use a pencil to write their answers so they appear to be the same, but this is not essential.

Students are each given a file card. The cards should all look the same.

Invite students to think of something they doubt their friends know about them. (Three example secrets: I have a scar on my elbow. I like to eat onion and peanut butter sandwiches. I won a baton twirling contest.) The statement should be true. Remind them that this will be shared with others so nothing too personal needs to be revealed.

The cards are collected and shuffled. Each student is given a card that is not their own. One person begins by standing and reading out the "secret" received. That person is challenged to guess the names of two people who might own that secret. After a moment or two the secret identity is revealed. That person then reads the secret he or she has received. The game continues until all secrets have been revealed.

Glyph Portraits

With thanks to Cathy Marks Krpan

A glyph is a simple picture or figure whose parts represent information about a given subject—hieroglyphics was picture writing used by Egyptians. Not only does this activity promote success for all learners, it promotes a sense of community as students work together and display their finished portraits in a classroom gallery display. The "Glyph Key" line master outline (page 29) is a sample that can be used with most age groups; it can be adapted in any way by changing or adding items.

Each student requires two sheets of colored paper, a pair of scissors, and a glue stick. Each student is also provided with a copy of the line master to help with interpreting their creation. This worksheet provides a key of symbols for the students to interpret. For example, a student whose family owns a cat would choose a diamond-shaped nose or a student who comes to school by car would choose cloud-shaped hair.

The teacher models the way the activity works by demonstrating which shape to make. (For example: "If I have a dog, which shape will I choose from the list to create a [nose] on the face?) Two or three demonstrations should suffice. Each student then creates an individual portrait by interpreting the symbols on the line master.

Once all faces have been completed, they can be put on display. To encourage interpretation of symbols, prompt students to look at a face and tell three things they learn about the person through their glyph creation.

It is recommended that the class be provided with only five or six colors (e.g., various shades of blue, bright neon colors, or primary and secondary colors only).

Glyph Portraits: Teaching Tips

- Although students are given only two colors to begin with, one of the colors should be a background. They can borrow colored scraps from their friends.
- For very young children, shapes can be pre-cut or the students can use stickers.
- A quicker activity might be to have the students draw their faces using the picture symbols.
- Paper plates or brown-paper bags can be used as a foundation for the glyph face.
- Offer additional items to the students who may finish the task early. For example, with more instructions, they can add "earrings" or a "necklace."
- Let students add an item to a category by creating a new symbol. For example, if they have a hamster, they can make up a symbol for that pet.
- In some cases, students may wish to use two symbols to create a feature (e.g., brother and sister).
- Prompt students to find an interesting way to display their name on their finished portrait.

Extensions

1. Students exchange faces and write five things they learn about their friend by looking at their glyph portrait.

2. Individuals write a short autobiography that includes some of the items from the glyph activity, for example, "Ten Things You Should Know About Me."

3. The glyph activity can be repeated at some time, by having the students create a whole-body figure. (One teacher used this activity for Halloween by having the students create monster faces.)

Glyph Key

Face Shape—Female/Male

Female

Male

Hair—Transportation to School

Car

Bus

Walk

Bicycle

Ears—Siblings

Has a brother

Has a sister

Has no brother or sister

Eyebrows—Birthday

January to April

May to August

September to December

Eyes—Favorite Food

Prefers pizza

Prefers chicken fingers

Prefers fish

Prefers vegetarian

Nose—Pets

Has a dog

Has a cat

Has a fish

Has no pets

Mouth—Favorite Drink

Juice

Water

Milk

4. Students create a non-glyph portrait of themselves using a different art medium, such as paint, markers, crayons, or oil pastels.

5. The activity can lead to sorting and classification. Students can group themselves according to similar features on their glyph faces (e.g., all those who have a brother).

6. Students can make a glyph face for a novel character or a notable figure from history.

Variation: To promote further interaction and collaboration, students can interview a friend to find out about the classmate's background, interests, and favorite things to do. Instead of making a self-portrait, each partner can make a glyph face for the friend.

Happy Birthday to Us!

Everyone has a birthday, and in any group community, we can find connections between those who were born in the same month and celebrate the birthdays of others. Many classroom bulletin-board displays are devoted to the birthdates of class members, and younger children can be given a special hat to wear on their special day.

Two birthday activities follow.

• *Birthday Line Up*

Birthday Line Up can be played in a variety of ways. Students arrange themselves in a line according to some criterion, such as height, alphabetically by first name, or alphabetically by last name. By standing in a line according to their birthdays from January to December, students can find out who was born in the same month and perhaps on the same day. In this way students create a "human graph" by finding which month is the most popular, which month has no birthdays represented, who in the class has the same birthday, and so on.

Extensions

1. Students can call out their birth dates. Encourage the students to listen carefully to the dates that have been called out and to think about people they know who might share similar birthdays as the ones that have been called out.

2. Students can be divided into two teams. As a task is called out, the teams can be challenged to arrange themselves in order before the other team.

3. Once students are arranged in lines, invite them to chat with a neighbor. Assign a topic, such as what the students did last night, how much television they watch, or whether they have read anything good lately.

• *Sharing "Birthdays," a poem by Sonja Dunn*

The poem "Birthdays" by Sonja Dunn includes everyone in the classroom community because everyone has a birthday. The poem can be shared in the following way:

1. Invite students raise their hands to designate their birthday month as the months of the year are called out.

2. Read the poem aloud and have students perform actions according to each couplet.

3. Have students read aloud the couplet that features their birthday month. If no one has a birthday in a particular month, either you can read it aloud or the whole class can say it in unison.

4. Prompt students to read aloud and perform the action for each couplet.

The poems in *All Together Now* by Sonja Dunn are perfect invitations for building community as students join in with others to chant, sing, or act out.

5. Rehearse the poem so that students are familiar with their parts. Students perform the poem by saying it chorally and adding gestures or movements to accompany the couplets. Ask the students to consider how they will stand or sit to perform this poem for others.

The poem "Birthdays," from the anthology *All Together Now* (Pembroke Publishers, 1999), is used with the express permission of the author, Sonja Dunn.

Birthdays

Hey, Hey
when's your Birthday?

Clap your hands
if it's January

Stamp your feet
if it's February

Shrug your shoulders
if it's March

If it's April
up you stand

Born in May
wave your hand

June's the month
To touch the sky

Fly around
if it's July

If it's August
blow your nose

In September
touch those toes

If your day is in October
start that day
by rolling over

In November
bend your knees

Here's December
you must freeze!

The Classroom as a Story Tribe: Sharing Personal Narratives

"The truth about stories is, that's all we are."

—Thomas King

The stories of our lives are swimming inside our heads. When we talk with others, these stories pop out of our mouths with the human need to share them with others. When we are at parties, at family gatherings, at dinner, in groups, on the street, in the hallways of the school, or in a mall, we tell stories about what has happened to us, to people we know, or to people we have heard or read about. Usually there is no specific instruction for sharing these memories. Sometimes a book, movie, or news report reminds us of things that have happened to us. Often when others tell their stories, ours are awakened, and when we are comfortable with the people we are with, we choose to tell these stories. Daniel Halpern writes:

> Stories are narratives well told: documents of our condition, seemingly limitless in their array of setting, tone, dialogue, and method of storytelling. It is via this ancient genre that the human spirit finds voice in its many tongues.

Teachers and their students have a treasure chest of stories waiting to be unlocked and shared. When students tell personal stories, they are not only choosing to reveal their life experiences to others, but they are building a dimension of who they are. Susan Engel, author of *The Stories Children Tell*, writes, "Each time a child describes an experience he or someone else has had, he constructs part of his past, adding to his sense of who he is and conveying that sense to others."

Narrative, according to Harold Rosen, is an important mode of thought that helps us to order our experiences and construct reality. It is the teacher's responsibility, therefore, to give time and attention for students to use narrative in their thinking, speaking, and writing in order to develop the full range of their cognitive abilities. Unless young people are given opportunities to tell their stories, they may never come to understand or give meaning to them. Oral narrative is a powerful way of validating one's own life to others. What may first be fleeting memories gain significance when told aloud.

Belarie Zatzman has helped us understand that storytelling includes a form of "witnessing." We have the obligation to retell our stories so that "there is a possibility of creating a landscape of intersection, where remembered/forgotten/ unknown/invented histories can live." Stories beget stories beget stories. Time must be allowed for students to recall stories, tell them to others, and find connections—to the text, to each other, and to the past. When teachers and students gather together in what David Booth calls a "story tribe," they validate each other's experiences as well as explore shared meanings. By sharing the stories, they are becoming part of a community where they are connected as they listen and respond to others.

Sometimes when a topic is offered, students may not be able to make an immediate personal connection, but they can be encouraged to tell stories about someone they know or perhaps read about. Personal narratives can emerge from

- children's literature that is shared with the class
- a word (e.g., *stitches, trip, seashore, lost, celebration, bully, prize, award*)
- a topic or question (see list next page)
- a story shared by someone else ("Your story reminds me of the time …")
- the recounting of an experience that recently happened in a student's life
- an artifact (e.g., a photograph, a spool of thread, a baby's bootie)

Several activities are outlined on the pages that follow.

From Word to Story

For this activity, students will work with others in a group to tell anecdotes, or stories that have happened to them, someone they know, or someone they have heard about. Once a group has chosen a topic from the list next page, a volunteer tells his or her story. Encourage students to provide as much detail as possible about the event and be prepared to answer questions from group members. Remind the students not to be surprised if the group takes a winding journey from the topic that members began with. Stories should continue to swim. Conversations should continue to flow.

A group can choose story prompts from the following list of words:

lost	picnics	danger
embarrassment	beaches	moving
stitches	airports	hospital
accidents	robberies	broken
surprises	museum	toy
celebrations	costumes	repairs
contests	zoos	birthdays
prizes	dreams	boats

"That Reminds Me …"

A group decides upon a topic from the list in "From Word to Story" to begin a conversation about personal experiences. One person is chosen to be the leader and tells a story. As the person completes the story, other group members put up a hand, saying, "That reminds me …" They begin to tell a story that has been inspired by a word or incident mentioned by the first storyteller. The activity continues, with each member volunteering to share an anecdote when reminded of one from another person's story.

A Topic a Day

Teachers may choose to introduce a topic such as one of those below to encourage students to share personal stories. Alternatively, the prompts could be recorded on paper, cut into strips, and put into an envelope, and a leader can choose a topic for the group to discuss:

- Describe the best vacation you've ever had.
- What teacher do you best remember? Why?
- Tell about the most memorable birthday you've ever had.
- Have you ever been in danger? What happened?
- Have you ever been afraid? Why?
- What special toys have been part of your life?
- What's the most special thing you've accomplished?
- Tell us about a team you have belonged to.
- Have you ever broken anything? What happened?
- Describe a time you repaired or built something.
- Talk about the book you best remember.
- Have you ever been admitted to the hospital? What happened?
- Tell about a time that you had to move.
- Describe a time that you were surprised.
- Tell us about a time a family pet or a friend's pet died.
- Describe a time when you had to be brave but it was very difficult.
- Tell us about a time when you had to forgive someone for what they did.
- Tell us a funny story about your family.
- Tell us about someone whom you admire. Why?
- Was there ever a time when you forgot something important? What happened?

Let the Artifacts Speak!

The class sits in a circle, and an object (e.g., a stone, a feather, an article of clothing, or a ring) is put in the centre. Students are given time to examine the object and respond to it personally. On a signal, invite students to tell the others what the object reminds them of and ask them to tell a story connected to the artifact.

Extension

Ask students to bring in objects connected to the theme or stories that they are studying. Have them tell personal stories about their objects and connect these to the texts.

Ten Ways Teachers Can Promote Oral Narrative

1. Share good books. When we make text-to-self connections to a book, we can consider it a good one.
2. Take the time to listen.
3. Allow digression.
4. Tell your own stories.
5. Organize groups in a variety of ways.
6. Initiate response before, during, and after reading a story.
7. Honor a variety of connections.
8. Ask questions.
9. Invite children to write stories and then read their favorite parts to others in small groups.
10. Do nothing: Let the stories wander through students' heads.

Encouraging Community Story Sharing Three Ways

Here are three contexts for community story sharing.

Whole-Class Sharing

A single topic is chosen for the whole class to discuss. Students turn to others around them to share stories. Volunteers can then share their stories with the whole class. Sometimes someone's story can trigger another story that students might want to share, even though a story may not be on the original topic.

Partner or Small-Group Sharing

Students work in small groups to tell stories based on a topic or question. Each student should have a chance to be storyteller. Students can be provided with a list of topics to choose from or can be assigned a topic. Encourage each storyteller to give as much detail and sensory description as possible to make a story come alive. Storytellers should also be encouraged to answer questions from group members.

Sharing in Double Circles

For this activity, students have a chance to share personal stories with half of the members of the class. Students form two circles (an inner and an outer). Facing one another, partners tell something that they did during the past weekend. Some conversations may be brief; some will last a few moments. After a short period, students are given a signal to change partners. Members of the inner circle remain where they are, while members of the outer circle move one place to the right. It is up to the teacher to suggest conversation topics such as an enjoyable meal or an embarrassing moment.

Options for further practice
1. When students return to their original partner, they can exchange stories that they heard from others during the activity.
2. Students can retell, in first-person voice, a story heard from a classmate.
3. Students can write about one story that they told others.
4. Students can gather stories by interviewing others in the school, in the community, or at home.

Hot Topic Discussions

With thanks to Wendie Gibbons

Just as we might ask students to share personal stories from their lives, students can be encouraged to offer opinions and share reactions to topics offered by the teacher (or another classmate). When this ritual is established in the class, it provides an opportunity for students to speak, to listen, and to participate cooperatively as a discussion unfolds. As students share their opinions as a community, they are also given an opportunity to witness viewpoints that may or may not be similar to their own. When a trusting community has been developed, students come to feel comfortable about sharing their feelings and telling stories they might have thought were private. In a safe space, students should be comfortable with their sharing.

Drama teacher Wendie Gibbons noticed that when her students were rehearsing plays, they would often share their highs and lows about day-to-day events. At the start of each rehearsal, students discussed topics and were often willing to be open and honest with one another about things that were happening in their lives and in the world. Wendie observed that this bonding exercise quickly established what kind of mood everyone was in and helped build authentic conversations. As a result, she decided to begin each of her classes with a Hot Topic discussion. Providing topic starters sometimes helped to massage students' personal memory story banks but also gave students the chance to expose their thoughts to an audience. As students shared views, they learned to articulate their thoughts, to actively listen, to ask appropriate questions, to seek clarification, and to hitchhike on each other's words.

For the teacher, this kind of discussion is a significant way to discover what is interesting and relevant in the lives of the students. As students build confidence to respond to a hot topic, they come to better respect and appreciate personal differences while developing a classroom dynamic that connects and cares.

Here are some prompts for hot topic discussions:

Inspiration for Hot Topics

A school event

A world event

A news event in the community

A television or radio program, movie, or play

A topic or question introduced by the teacher

A topic or question introduced by a student

- How was your weekend?
- Would you rather be beautiful or smart?
- What would you do if you won a large lottery?
- Will there ever be world peace?
- If I could change one thing about myself …
- If I could change one thing about the world …
- If you could have one superhuman power, what would it be?
- My favorite comfort food is …
- The color that best represents me is …
- If I could be any animal in the world, I'd be …
- If I could be any number in the world, I'd be …
- Money buys happiness.
- Here's what I expect my life to be like in 10 years (in 20 years).
- A book that everyone in the world should read is …
- What's on your iPod?
- Girls talk more than boys.
- If I knew someone was being bullied, …
- A good teacher is …
- I like (don't like) my name because …
- Homework matters.

A Caveat: Students are likely not going to fully share their personal stories unless they feel some connection to each other. It is important to take the time to explore and share personal identity stories. These events can take place many times throughout the year. Remember that discussions about personal identity should not be rushed. They take a certain amount of sensitivity and awareness on the part of all participants. Students can make decisions about how much they want to communicate about their personal history and identity.

"The Important Thing About Me Is ..."

Tell students that this is an activity in which they will have an opportunity to share those unique personal qualities that they believe make them who they are. It allows them to articulate things that others might not have known about them and to find ways of valuing difference. It also encourages them to think collectively about issues of diversity in the classroom so that a level of trust is built among them. The exercise is meant to hone students' skills of self-reflection as well as help everyone to value and celebrate difference. Significant time is needed for this activity because the conversations that develop require active listening and sensitive responses.

You also need to be aware of those students who are not easily accepted into a group. Try rearranging the members of groups to make sure that there is sufficient support for everyone.

Invite students to bring in a photograph of one or more members of their family, a favorite family recipe, a picture that they might have drawn or painted when they were a young child, a family memento, or anything else that has some kind of personal significance and that they might be able to talk about in class. Whatever they bring in must be durable and not so precious that it might break and cause a huge sense of loss to the owner. The artifact needs to have some sort of story attached to it. When students bring their artifact to class, they need to have it covered up in some way—in an envelope, in a box, or wrapped in newspaper.

Have students, in groups of four or five, decide who will be the first person to talk about their object. Each student will be given an opportunity to present an object to the group by describing it, talking about its importance to the individual or the family, and allowing people to see it closely, pass it around, and ask questions about it. At the end of the presentation, each student explains why this object is important.

After all of the individuals have presented, create a word wall and sort the artifacts.

Possible Artifacts

Photographs

Recipes

Letters

Documents

Books

Writing

Invite the students to consider what these artifacts have taught them about who is in the room. Have them complete this statement: "We are people who ..." Answers might include the following: come from other places in the world, have extended families, speak many languages, value our grandparents, miss our home countries.

Students can deepen their understanding of their classroom community by discussing these questions:

- How are we all the same? How are we different?
- Today what did we learn about ourselves that we did not know before?

- Why is it important to acknowledge these similarities and differences among us?
- What impact will this knowledge have on our cooperative work together as a class?
- When we do exercises like this, what do we learn about ourselves and others?
- How might you feel or act differently because of the new knowledge that you acquired through this exercise?
- What kinds of communication and interaction in the group might change because of what we just shared together? Why do you think that might happen?
- How can listening to personal stories help us learn to understand, appreciate, and respect each other?

And here are some questions for independent student reflection:

- Was this an easy or a difficult exercise for you to do? What factors made it easy or difficult?
- Were you surprised by the reaction of your group to you and your important object?
- Did you learn something about another person that you did not know about before?
- Why is it that others see us differently from how we see ourselves?

When the Teacher Reads Aloud: A Community-Building Event

Many, but not all, of children's first encounters with books in their homes are while listening to a caring adult reading aloud to them. Whether the adult is a parent, relative, librarian, or early years teacher, young children become engaged with the book, looking at the illustrations and hearing the cadences of the poem, story, or informational text being read aloud. The pleasure of enjoying a book with someone significant in their lives can continue throughout the school years. Teachers can build on the expectations established in many children's preschool years by reading aloud daily to students of any age.

Reading to our students models both fluent reading and a love of reading. Students are introduced to texts they might not otherwise encounter when teachers read aloud to them. Hearing a book read expands students' vocabulary and their familiarity with a variety of sentence structures and ideas. When reading aloud, teachers should be familiar with the content of the text and communicate their enthusiasm for it. The primary goal of reading aloud is to foster young people's enjoyment and understanding of the text. When questions are asked to encourage students to share their thoughts, opportunity is given to deepen understanding, clarify difficult concepts or relationships, or encourage emotional response to the book.

The selection of literature to read to children depends on the students' ages and attention spans, and on their interests and abilities. The books that we choose to read aloud can be integrated into the curriculum and can lead to meaningful talk, writing, visual arts, or drama activities. When reading aloud becomes a ritual in the classroom, students not only develop their own tastes in books, but their own reading can be enriched as they choose to read other books by an author, in a genre, or to seek information about a topic offered by the read-aloud.

Whether they are listening to a picture book, chapter book, novel, non-fiction selection, or poetry, reading-aloud time provides children with an opportunity to stretch their reading tastes and abilities. We are often asked how we select books to read aloud to our students. Ultimately, if the adult connects to the book with enthusiasm, then it is worthy of sharing with the students (who may or may not be as enthusiastic in their review of the book). A teacher's enthusiasm matters, and the book that we choose to read aloud should be worthy of time spent by the readers and listeners who form our audience.

It is not uncommon to want to find someone to talk to in order to share our impressions of a movie, play, or television show we've just seen or a book we've just read. Such conversations enable us to sort out what we think and to distance ourselves a little from the immediacy of the experience. Aidan Chambers, author of *Tell Me: Children, Reading and Talk*, explains that such conversations involve the sharing of enthusiasms, the sharing of puzzles, and the sharing of connections. When all the members of a class have read or listened to the same book, the sharing allows them to rub ideas and opinions against those of other members of the group, and can often lead them together to insights they might never have discovered alone.

"Reading aloud is an activity that builds community in the classroom because there is common listening but varied response. The texts allow students to share their varied responses and grow in their understanding that we all bring our different selves to a text and therefore respond differently."

—Aidan Chambers, *Tell Me: Children, Reading and Talk*

Read-Aloud Books Centred on Caring

Ten Picture Books
Croza, Laurel (Illus. Matt James). *I Know Here.*
Graham, Bob. *How to Heal a Broken Wing.*
Kajikawa, Kimiko (Illus. Ed Young). *Tsunami!*
Light, John (Illus. Lisa Evans). *The Flower.*
Lightfoot, Gordon (Illus. Ian Wallace). *The Canadian Railroad Trilogy.*
Muth, Jon J. *The Three Questions.*
Viorst, Judith (Illus. Lane Smith). *Lulu and the Brontosaurus.*
Wersba, Barbara (Illus. Donna Diamond). *Walter: The Story of a Rat.*
Wells, Rosemary. *Yoko's World of Kindness.*
Wild, Margaret (Illus. Ron Brooks). *Fox.* (Also: *Harry & Hopper*)

Ten Novels
Avi. *The End of the Beginning.* (Sequel: *A Beginning, A Muddle and an End*)
Boyne, John. *Noah Barleywater Runs Away.*
Clements, Andrew. *Extra Credit.*
Di Camillo, Kate. *The Miraculous Journey of Edward Toulane* (Also: *The Magician's Elephant*)
Gardiner, John Reynolds. *Stone Fox.*
Morpurgo, Michael. *War Horse* (Also: *Born to Run* and *An Elephant in the Garden*)
Hess, Patrick (Conceived by Siobhan Dowd). *A Monster Calls.*
Oppel, Kenneth. *Half Brother.*
Spinelli, Jerry. *Loser* (Also: *Eggs* and *Maniac Magee*)
Walliams, David. *Mr. Stink.*

Promoting Student Leadership in the Elementary Classroom

by Amy Craze

Amy Craze is an elementary teacher in the Toronto District School Board. She is a graduate of the Initial Teacher Education program at the Ontario Institute of Education, University of Toronto. Amy has certified qualifications as a drama specialist as well as Lower Elementary Teaching for Montessori. She has worked as a singer/songwriter but now enjoys her new job as a mom!

Six weeks into the school year, I had accepted a job to teach a Grade 1/2 classroom. I had been warned that my new class would be "challenging" considering that they had gone through six teachers within the past six weeks. Fresh out of a program in Initial Teacher Education, I was eager and optimistic to take on the journey. Leading up to my first day, I spent countless hours organizing the class and outlining a daily program that I was sure would make things run smoothly. When it came time to greet my new students, I felt amply prepared—and optimistic!

When the children arrived, I went over a list of routines that I had thoughtfully laid out and surprisingly, I met little opposition on that first morning. I was left wondering why anyone would find this group challenging. Based on our early day success, I decided to try an unstructured painting lesson with the students in the afternoon. My enthusiastic smile seemed to vanish when I found 21 students, each wearing white tops as part of their uniform, engaged in a paint fight.

So much for careful planning!

This chaotic experience (and my subsequent years of teaching) made me determined to create a learning community in my classroom that fosters respect for one another and the classroom itself. I quickly realized that it takes more to build a classroom than the teacher listing rules and the students diligently following them—students needed to be part of the process. The guiding principle of my classroom has since become: "We can all learn from one another."

Ways to Build Student Leadership in a Primary Classroom

It is one thing to have a banner on the wall—for example, *Everyone is a teacher, if we choose to let them be*—and another to put a banner into action. The following outline provides six key practices that I consider important to build student leadership and to build a community that works for all.

1. Creating a mission statement

The very first day of the school year, when I gather my students on the carpet for community time, we develop our classroom mission statement. The mission statement is always a variation of the following three rules.

- Let's take turns when we talk.
- Look and listen when others speak.
- Don't touch others without permission to do so.

I then proceed to lead the students through the following scenarios:

- What would happen if we spoke all at the same time?
- If it is our turn to teach something to the class, do you think the people in the audience would learn anything if they are staring into space instead of looking at the person who is talking?
- If we are touching the person in front of us or playing with their shoe laces what might happen?

2. Learning from each other: More than a slogan

I plan the first introductory curriculum unit of the year to provide a framework for the students to recognize and to celebrate "Our Differences." A number of integrated reading, writing, and arts activities, including self-portraits, stories about our names, All About Me books, and cooperative games, are designed to demonstrate that each of us is a unique individual and as such, special. Together, the boys and girls examine what would happen if we were all exactly the same. What if we all looked the same, solved math problems the exact same way, and all wrote the exact same stories? The students inevitably come to the conclusion that it would be a pretty boring classroom if we were all so similar. Because we are all different, we all have something to learn from one another.

3. Team building: Classroom responsibilities

Assigning all the children a classroom responsibility every week instills in them a sense of pride and ownership of the classroom. Roles may include the following: attendance monitor, lunch bin monitor, handout monitor, light and door monitors, and pet monitor. Outlining clear expectations for each responsibility as it is introduced enables children to succeed with confidence. From week to week, students can experience a variety of different roles, each giving them responsibility and a taste of being a leader.

Three roles are outlined below:

Line leader: This person prepares the class to walk down the hall in a respectful way so that collectively students act as leaders and do not disturb other classes that are working.

Table monitor: This person is in charge of ensuring that the group works as a team to tidy their table before coming to the carpet for group activities. After every lesson, the monitor is in charge of collecting the folders or handouts and putting them in the appropriate bins. At the end of the day, each table monitor fills in a checklist.

Music monitor: This monitor is in charge of playing all the music to accompany transitions throughout the day. Putting on the morning song is the signal for the students to tidy their desks, push in their chairs, and come to the carpet for Calendar time each morning.

4. Establishing predictable routines

When the classroom is set up using predictable routines, it becomes easy for the students to learn these routines and lead them independently, taking on more responsibility and challenging routines as the year progresses.

Morning and end-of-day routines: Outside of my classroom, there are two posters that clearly mark, using pictures and words, the morning and end-of-day routines for the students. Each morning as I greet the students, I remind them what to do upon their entrance to class. By second term, although the students know what they are expected to do, I assign a different student each day to take on this role and remind the students of these classroom routines.

Calendar: A 25-minute, 13-step routine, Calendar combines activities from the various math, writing, and science strands that are taught throughout the year. These mini-lessons are made engaging to the students by incorporating drama, movement, and music. First term I lead Calendar for the students and model each step; by second term the students take on this responsibility.

Mathematics lessons: Each mathematics lesson I teach in class is designed in a way that it builds off the lesson before. Using this format, each lesson includes a review component from the day before.

Sharing time: After Writing Workshop, science and mathematics lessons, or Reading Workshop, students are given the opportunity to share what they have learned with the class. This sharing time acts to consolidate each lesson and build confidence in each child.

5. Introducing a caring vocabulary

When giving the students the opportunity to take on a teaching or leadership role in front of the class, it is important to offer them appropriate vocabulary to be successful. Although many of the students may internalize your classroom management vocabulary, I find it important to teach the students what I say to ensure that their audience will be ready to listen attentively to them. The following script is an important ritual that helps children get the attention of others: "Please look to your left and your right and if you are sitting next to someone you are going to talk to, touch, or be distracted by, please make a good choice and move in 5…4…3…2…1. Thank you for making good choices."

6. Sharing Happy Monday Messages

Every Monday during Calendar time, I read a Happy Monday Message to each child in my class. This message focuses on a newly developed skill that the child has developed, an initiative taken in his or her work, or positive character traits exhibited in the class-room. In doing so, it celebrates and reinforces the positive leadership roles each student takes in the classroom and encourages others to do the same.

Happy Monday Messages at Work

In my first year teaching I worked with a student named Evan. One morning, Evan tried to sneak into class before the bell had rung. I told him that if he were to come into the class, he could help his fellow students by un-stacking the chairs. He did so a tad reluctantly. The following Monday, when I read aloud each child's Happy Monday Message, I thanked Evan for coming in and un-stacking each child's chair in the classroom. I thanked him for his kindness and for caring for the classroom community. That week, Evan took it upon himself to come and un-stack the class-room chairs each day. He did so until the very last day of school, but this was not all. Each morning after he had un-stacked our classroom chairs, Evan went to our neighboring classrooms to see if he could un-stack their chairs as well. By the end of the year Evan had taken the initiative to un-stack the chairs of the four main classrooms on the first floor. That year, Evan proved himself as an inspirational, caring leader. He demonstrated how far a little positivity can go!

That first year was a year of exploration, discovery, and reflection. Now that several years have passed since that first day, I would say that my classroom has since become an orga-nized environment with predictable structures, routines, and expectations that the stu-dents and I work hard to establish—together. With a structure in place, the students are able to internalize the classroom routines and expectations, and proudly take on various leadership roles. Empowering the students to take on leadership roles has been signifi-cant in helping every student gain the opportunity to become a leader, a teacher.

Engaging the Disengaged

by Ramon San Vincente

Formerly a course director at York University, Faculty of Education, Ramon San Vincente is now an instructional leader with the Equitable and Inclusive Schools Department of the Toronto District School Board. Throughout his 12-year teaching career, Ramon has displayed a passion for integrating the arts, creating spaces for the exploration of youth culture, working specifically with marginalized students and communities, and challenging existing practices that continue to produce inequitable outcomes for students in schools.

I believe that the greatest professional development I have received as a teacher has come through the mentorship work that I have done with our most disadvantaged and disengaged students. Mentorship, not only as a co-curricular or extracurricular program, but as a pedagogical approach, has proven to be a foundation upon which to build what was my ultimate goal as a teacher: a caring, collaborative, and inclusive environment whereby all of us could develop and excel intellectually, emotionally, and socially. My approach to mentorship has been grounded in three principles: (1) caring about the whole child (not just academics), (2) emphasizing relationship building, and (3) investing time outside of formal instructional time. The relationships we were able to collaboratively build through mentorship offered me a clearer window into the complexities of my students' lives, both their challenges and their assets.

Mentorship became a transformational opportunity for me. It allowed me to refine my pedagogical practice, challenge preconceived notions I had about certain families and communities, build relationships with parents and community, engage in curriculum that was relevant and grounded in a more in-depth understanding of the lives of my students—all within an approach that was less traditional and more responsive. My experiences running a mentorship program for disengaged boys helped me to transform my teaching practice to be more inclusive and allowed me to become more aware of how to construct comfortable spaces for collaboration and community in my classroom.

My journey into mentorship began in the second year of my teaching career when I decided to be proactive about what was an obvious reality in my classroom, throughout the school, and, I'm sure, across the board. Certain groups of students were highly disengaged, frequently in the office for misbehavior, often suspended, and ultimately on a path towards dropping out. These students were the centre of the conversation at the lunch table in the staff room and at the bottom of the wish list for the teaching staff as we conceived of our dream class. In my particular school, these students happened to be predominantly boys and predominantly from racialized communities, but this marginalized group exists in every school in different forms.

My strategy with this group was … well, I didn't really have one. My thinking was simply that these were the most at-risk children and that they were often denied the type of caring adult connection within the school (and, in some cases, also outside of the school) that they needed if they were to have a chance at success. I also felt that, if I could connect with these students, I would gain valuable insight into the challenges and barriers they faced, information that would help me to successfully program for them, but also for all students. Finally, I felt that, if I could make connections with the children who were the most difficult to reach, making connections with others would be really easy. So, I began without a plan but with the intent to take one small step at a time.

The Building of a Community

As risky as it might seem, I decided to get a group of these boys together just to spend some time in each other's company and have some informal dialogue. This process was made easier by the fact that I had already, without an intentional plan, begun reaching out and forming connections with many students outside my immediate class. I greeted students in the hallway, attempted to learn their names, ate lunch in the student cafeteria once a week, and went outside at lunch time just to hang out for a few minutes. Thus, when we came together that first time, it was fairly seamless and comfortable. I wrote the following about our first meeting in a 2011 article titled "Learning Through Mentorship: Accessing Opportunities to Support Boys":

> I remember our first meeting sitting in a circle on the tattered couches in the back of my grade 8 classroom. It was myself and about 8–10 boys who I had invited to meet with me over lunch. While there was no official selection process to determine who was to be invited ... I had deliberately chosen the boys who were getting the most negative attention in the building ... As we slouched on the couches enjoying our break from the daily routines of school, the moments of silence in the conversation quickly began to dissipate as we became more comfortable discussing whatever was on their minds. From gangs, to girls to guns, to how they felt disrespected in the school, I focused on listening to their thoughts and observing their interactions with each other. Every once in a while I shared a thought, experience or perspective on the issue but my contribution was minimal. I felt like what was most important to this process was the trust we developed knowing that what was shared in that room stayed in that room. This informal gathering on the couches of room 106 became a weekly experience that, based on their regular attendance, the boys seemed to truly value.

As our relationship grew, so did the activities that we became involved in. Homework help, dominoes, film viewings, the creation of their own hip hop song, a community-run martial arts program, camping trips, and lunchtime walks to the park were some of our activities. These activities were based on the identified interests and needs of the students. Eventually, this work meant connecting with the parents of these boys to let them know what we were up to and bringing in community members or agencies to run programming. A key component of this was also putting the boys in leadership roles whenever possible. Whether organizing a school assembly, working on the school garden, or their taking on some other position of responsibility, I felt, it was important for them, for me, and particularly for the other staff and students to begin to see the boys in a different light.

A significant part of my learning through this process came in the realization that I couldn't do this work alone and be as effective as I needed to be. Thus, by the second year, I was collaborating with two other teachers who helped to facilitate our conversations and collectively plan programming. Our collaboration had the effect of increasing staff buy-in and allowing us to bounce ideas off each other—an approach that ultimately enhanced our practice.

The main focus in our program was on building strong relationships and listening in a non-judgmental way to the concerns and circumstances of these students. This approach seemed to allow us to build the level of trust that was necessary for a caring, collaborative, and inclusive environment, one that I later learned was easily transferable to the work I did in my own Grade 7 classroom as I worked to build community.

What I Learned About Engaging Students

So, what exactly did I learn from co-running this mentorship program that I could then use to build a culture of caring, collaboration, and inclusiveness throughout my teaching practice?

I learned the value of taking the time to include students. Acknowledging them in the hallways, asking about their evening, sharing a meal, providing a non-judgmental ear to listen to their concerns about life both in and out of school, and walking the school grounds with them for 10 minutes at lunch were all manageable steps I could take daily. Approaching students this way made an astronomical difference for the students and for myself in the classroom.

This approach meant a lot for me in my teaching practice. It meant I had now made a connection with students that I didn't directly teach and that many students knew that I cared about them beyond their schoolwork. It also meant that classroom management was much easier because I had built relationships with many of the most challenging students even before they came to my class in September, that parents had heard of the work that I was doing and were even more open to collaborating with me to support learning for their children. Through this process, I had a better sense of the strengths and challenges that existed in the community. I had found people with whom I could connect with for support. I also believe that by connecting with the most challenged children in the building, I unintentionally sent the message that I would be here to support them all, even those who had an unfavorable reputation with their teachers and with the school.

In essence, the professional learning that occurred through this journey encouraged me to switch from the motto "all students can learn" to "all students will learn." I find the latter to be more meaningful and full of truth for, beyond stating the obvious about our abilities as humans, it is a call to action. As an educator, I am responsible for the success or failure of my students, and so I must ensure that my approach and practices facilitate success for all. For me, this goal did not mean that all students would achieve the same results in their various subjects, but rather, that all students would experience significant growth in their academic performance, their desire to engage, and their self-confidence.

How Does My Approach Translate to Student Success?

By choosing to include the experiences, perspectives, and cultures of my students and their communities, I observed that my students, on a whole, were now more connected to their educational experience. They talked more positively about school, they looked forward to hanging out in our classroom, they desired to engage and improve their academic performance, and many of them desired to maintain some form of connection long after they had moved on from their middle-school experience.

Recently, I reconnected with a former student who had been severely at-risk when I first met him in my Grade 7 classroom. He was now going on to post-graduate studies. I asked the pressing question: "So, what actually made the difference for you?" He quickly responded, "A few teachers who cared."

This is why my experience in the mentorship program and subsequent transference of this learning to my classroom I present as my greatest professional development. It taught me how to care and provide an inclusive and comfortable space in a way that was meaningful, manageable, and ultimately transformative.

Chapter 2

Building Communication

*School should be a place where we can hear the full
sound of the conversation of humankind.*
—David Booth

There are many ways that we can work together to help students learn to communicate more effectively. The first thing to do is to help students become generally interested in who is in the room and what they have to contribute. Believing that the work is important and buying into it is an ongoing challenge, but an essential ingredient to a caring classroom culture.

The Nature of Communication

Nearly everyone thinks that communication is about talking, but it is also about listening. Listening to what everyone has to say is as important as talking. It is difficult to insist on students listening, but it is one of the key aspects of a caring and communicative classroom—the capacity to acknowledge other voices and to be aware of the people who are too shy to speak or who feel that they have nothing to contribute.

Communication is about conveying something to a particular audience: sharing in small groups, presenting to the class, performing to a large audience. It's about talking, writing, texting, and drawing. And it's about using social media—text and image together; using visual media; and using gesture and body language.

Communicating, an essential part of being human, begins at birth. Students need to learn how to communicate with others. In doing so they learn an enormous amount about life skills: they learn how to find appropriate ways to convey important messages and how to be precise and accurate. Often this takes a whole lot of practice, but these skills can be taught in fun ways. All of this is connected to thinking, and logic can be a lot of fun to play around with!

Students need to communicate about things that are relevant to them: that have some personal significance. ELL students are challenged to tell us about what they are learning in their new language. It takes a long time for students to gain total fluency and the steps along the way are often uneven. In a caring classroom, a fair bit of patience and encouragement are required. Grouping students in such a way that they help each other learn both the content and the language is crucial.

Communication is related to thinking. It is nuanced. It is connected to our ability to be critical about what we are saying and hearing. Good communicators are flexible. If they cannot explain it one way, they try another way. Consider the questions that follow:

- What do I think about this?
- Why am I thinking this way?
- Can I rethink?
- Can I shift my thinking and communicate differently?

Games That Encourage Talk

These games foster communication among students. They allow them time to listen carefully to one another, to talk, to laugh, and to have fun. They are meant to help students pay attention to the language they are using. They also encourage students to interact with as many people as possible in the classroom—in partners, in small groups, and as a whole. Students work with word language and body language, honing their communication skills.

The games encourage students to look more critically at human interactions and to talk about their intellectual and emotional responses to these interactions in an honest and open fashion. Students share opinions and debate choices as they work together, building off one another's ideas. They find language appropriate to the situation and encourage one another to excel and contribute.

Fortunately/Unfortunately

Ask the students to sit in groups of five or six. Have them number themselves off (1-2-3-4-5). Student 1 starts a story beginning with the line "Last night, as I was coming home from work, my car broke down." Student 2 continues the story but must start her part with the word "fortunately." Student 3 continues the story but begins his sentence with "unfortunately." The words are used alternately as the story is told by each member of the group. Encourage the group members to go around the circle at least twice. Ask for volunteers to share the gist of the story with the class.

Here is how one story might go. You might want to use this as an example for students to understand the exercise a bit better.

1: Last night, as I was coming home from work, my car broke down.
2: Fortunately, I had my cell phone.
3: Unfortunately, when I called home, no one answered.
4: Fortunately, I was close to a gas station.
5: Unfortunately, the gas station attendant was locking up when I arrived.
6: Fortunately, he listened to my story.
7: Unfortunately, he was rushing to the hospital because his wife was in labor.
8: Fortunately, he gave me a lift to the nearest bus station.
9: Unfortunately, I didn't have any money to buy a ticket.
10: Fortunately, the ticket agent took pity on me and lent me some money.

Are You Thinking What I'm Thinking?

With thanks to Jack Bevington

"We have two ears and one mouth so that we can listen twice as much as we speak."
—Epictetus

To demonstrate how this game works, have two volunteers sit in chairs in front of the class or in the centre of a circle. Tell the two volunteers to each think of a word, preferably a noun. On a signal, each player says the word out loud, for example, "computer" and "puzzle."

Direct the players to think of a word that comes to mind when they hear those words. Players do not say the words out loud, unless told to do so. On a signal, each player says the word that came to mind, for example, "game" and "challenge." The game continues, until each player says the same word simultaneously—the challenge is to do so in as few turns as possible. Encourage players to be spontaneous in their word choices. They do not have to explain the reason for their choices.

Here is a sample of how the game might go:

A: Computer.
B: Puzzle.
REFEREE: Think of a word that connects to "computer" and "puzzle."
A: Game.
B: Challenge.
REFEREE: Think of a word that connects "game" and "challenge."
A: Olympics.
B: Hockey.
REFEREE: Think of a word that connects "Olympics" and "hockey."
A: Score.
B: Goalie.
REFEREE: Think of a word that connects "score" and "goalie."
A: Puck!
B: Puck!

Variation #1: Once the class is familiar with the game, students can play in groups of three, with one person being the referee.

Variation #2: For a further challenge, the game can be played with three players offering words.

Drawing Game

Drawing Game provides students with the opportunity to demonstrate effective oral communication skills by giving and following directions accurately. To begin, students find a partner and sit back to back. Alternatively, this game can be played in small groups with one person chosen to be the leader.

With paper and pencil, a leader begins by drawing a simple picture. The leader then gives directions that will allow the partner to duplicate the picture. At the end of the game, partners compare their creation with the original design.

Extensions
1. Students make up their own designs and rather than give oral instructions, write precise directions for others to follow.
2. Partners take turns giving instructions on how to draw a monster. (For example: #1: draw a large circle in the centre of the page; #2: put a triangle in the centre of the circle; #1: add two large eyes shaped like cherries on top of the circle.) After each instruction, both partners draw what has been requested. Each partner can give 8 to 10 instructions. At the end of the activity, students compare their drawings to determine their success in giving or following directions.

Eleven Fingers

Students sit in groups of three. Players chant the following: "North, South, East, West," the signal for each member of the group to show any number of fingers from one hand. Players count the total number of fingers shown. A closed fist

To make the activity easier, listeners may be allowed to question their partners. To make the activity more difficult, instructions for more intricate designs can be given and no questions allowed.

counts as zero. The object of the game is to show a total of 11 fingers. Players cannot confer with each other. The first team to complete the task successfully five times or the team with the most successful completions within a given time limit can be declared the winner. A simple extension is for players to use both hands to count: the challenge is to show 23 fingers in total.

Rabbit in a Knapsack

An empty knapsack (or bag or box) is used for this activity, which can be done with the large group or in small groups. The knapsack is given to one of the students in the group. The person who hands the knapsack over asks: "Why have you got a rabbit in your knapsack?" The student has to think of a convincing or original reason to explain why the rabbit is there and be prepared to answer questions raised by the rest of the group. The interview should last between three and five minutes. The person who was interviewed then hands the knapsack over to another player with the same question, only this time another object is mentioned, for example: "Why have you got a hammer in your knapsack?" "Why have you got a pineapple in your knapsack?"

Scrambled Sentences

1. To begin, choose a sentence from a newspaper or a novel. The sentence is written on the board, but the words are not presented in the correct order. Challenge the students to work in pairs to determine what they think the correct sentence should be.

> *funny The thing about a bone is not that it is bone all at funny at*
> The funny thing about a funny bone is that it is not a bone at all.

2. Students can work alone or in pairs to create a scrambled sentence, writing the sentence on a piece of paper. Students exchange scrambled sentences and challenge each other to put the sentence in original order as quickly as possible.

Variation #1: Students are given five or six words that have been scrambled. Repeat the above activity, challenging them to unscramble the words correctly. For example, they could unscramble these color words: *genre, aoerng, iinodg, ileotv, bwnor.*

Variation #2: Combine the scrambled words and scrambled sentence activity so that the words of the sentence are scrambled as well as the order of the words.

Variation #3: Cut up lines from a free-verse poem and place them in an envelope. Challenge the students to arrange the lines in an order that they think was originally used by the poet.

Let's Discuss It

Students are organized into groups of six. Each member is assigned a number from 1 to 6. Two dice are thrown to indicate the students to participate in a conversation. A third dice is used to show the topic for the pair to discuss for a minimum of three minutes. Students can choose which of the two topics they would like to discuss under the main heading. Other members can eventually join in the conversation by asking a question, or contributing to the topic. When 6 is thrown, students can choose topics of their own to discuss.

#1—VIDEO GAMES

Video games are not very educational.
Some video games are becoming too violent.

#2—MONEY

Buying lottery tickets is a waste of money.
The government needs to better prioritize its spending.

#3—ART

Looking at nature, there is no need for art.
Too much money is spent on buying art.

#4—FASHION

You can never have too many clothes.
No one should tell you what to wear.

#5—SPORTS

There is too much violence in sports.
It's not if you win or lose; it's how you play the game.

#6—FREE CHOICE

Variation: Students can write down topics for discussion and put them on file cards. The group collects the file cards and places them face down. Each card is given a number. The activity is repeated.

File Card Choices: Teaching Tips

File, or index, cards have proved to be very useful in our classrooms and are a convenient way to have students record their thoughts independently before sharing them out loud with a partner or with a group.

- File cards are small, so students don't feel intimidated about having to write a lot.
- File cards come in different sizes. With the same activity students might write a longer response and then eventually move to a shorter response (or vice versa). Some file cards are blank and some have lines so they are useful for both visual and written activities.
- File cards come in different colors, so they are useful for helping to organize groups. Students can meet with others who have the same color of card or different-colored cards.
- Written responses on file cards are useful to prepare students for discussion. Sometimes students are invited to write a short answer to a question or response to a text.
- Students are given a list of prompts to record their answers which will be shared with others. Students can be given permission to omit an answer if something doesn't come to mind for a prompt.

Deal Me In

Students sit in groups of five or six. Each group is given a deck of cards or one suit from a deck of cards which is spread out on the table face down. Each person, in turn, selects one card from the deck and answers the following questions depending on the card that has been chosen. Once played, cards can be returned to the pile. The game continues with students each having a chance to choose a card about four times.

Ace	Tell about the #1 book you have ever read.
2	Describe the most interesting part of your day 2 day.
3	Name 3 places you would like to visit.
4	Tell about the best gift you received 4 a birthday.
5	Name 5 movies you've enjoyed watching.
6	Share a memory of when you were 6 years old.
7	What is your favorite day of the week?
8	Describe the best meal you ever 8.
9	What would you do if you were given 9 thousand dollars?
10	What do you think or hope you will be doing 10 years from now?
Jack	picks another card
Queen	asks the person on right any question
King	is allowed to pass

Word Games

Crosswords, word searches, and other word puzzles are popular pastimes for many people young and old. Often when we can't figure out an answer, we turn to someone else for help. When working with others to play word games, students will have the opportunity to develop vocabulary, use logic, test spelling skills, and share ideas with others. They can play one or more of the games below with or without a piece of paper. By following the instructions, they can work with others out loud to solve the problems of attacking words.

• *I Packed My Knapsack*

Each player adds one item that is packed in the knapsack. The game is cumulative so as the brainstorming continues, each player must list in order the items that have been previously mentioned. A further challenge is to list words alphabetically, as two syllables, or on a particular theme or topic (e.g., animals, food, colors).

PLAYER 1: I packed my knapsack with an apple.
PLAYER 2: I packed my knapsack with an apple and a banana
PLAYER 3: I packed my knapsack with an apple, a banana, and a comic.

• *Scrambled Words*

A long word, such as *neighborhood, caterpillars, valentines,* or *conversational,* is decided upon. The players can compete to see how many new words of three letters or more they can spell rearranging the letters of the word. A letter can be used only as many times as it appears in the word. The player (or pairs of players) with the most words wins the game. You might wish to score the game by giving 1 point for three-letter words, 3 points for four- or five-letter words, and 5 points for words six letters or over.

• *Ping Pong Words*

This game is played with each person in turn calling out a word quickly according to a topic that is suggested by one group member. This person, assigned the role of caller and timer (to begin, we suggest a time limit of two minutes), suggests a topic for the word game: How many words can you spell that end in *y*? have double consonants? have three syllables? include the letter *x*? are six letters only? begin with *o*? end with *-tion*?

An alternate way to play this game is to work in teams of two or three. You can have a competition to see which team has the most words on the list for the topic that has been assigned.

Word Race can be made more challenging by setting a rule that the words be of two syllables, three syllables, five letters exactly, more than five letters, proper nouns only, or adjectives, for example. When one minute is up, the second player is given one point for each word he or she named.

- **Word Race**

Groups of five or six sit in a circle. Player 1 names a letter (excluding *x y z*)—*l*, for example. On a signal the player on the right must, within one minute, name as many words as he or she can think of that begin with that letter. As the words are called—*lemon, lamp, licence, leader*—the first player counts them while keeping track of the time. Plurals and repetitions are not acceptable. Then it is player 2's turn to time the player on the right by calling out another letter of the alphabet. The game proceeds in this way until all the players have taken a turn, each with a different letter. The one who gets the most words wins the game.

- **Choosy Charles**

In groups, one person as the caller announces: "Let's choose a gift for Choosy Charles who doesn't like the letter *e*. I will give Choosy Charles a lamp. What will you give Choosy Charles?"

Each player, in turn, names a gift for Choosy Charles. In this case, the name of the gift should not have the letter *e* in it. If the player names a gift already mentioned or identifies an item that includes the letter *e*, he or she is eliminated.

PLAYER 2: I will give Choosy Charles a candy.
PLAYER 3: I will give Choosy Charles a flower.
LEADER: You're out! Flower has an *e*.

The game can be repeated by naming other vowels or consonants that need to be avoided. Another challenge is to play the game by announcing two letters that Choosy Charles does not like. These letters can be two vowels, two consonants, or a vowel and a consonant.

Introducing Oral Communication Events

Talk is thought out loud. Strong oral language skills are essential to a student's social, emotional, and intellectual development. Students thrive and expand their communicative competence when they are encouraged to "talk themselves into understanding" whether it be about a text, a visual, a topic of interest, or a thought shared by others. Oral language proficiency depends on students speaking to a range of audiences, in a variety of contexts about things of significance to them. Social talk is a natural way for students to have conversations, but in our classrooms, we need to offer events that give structure to student conversations. We need to provide opportunities for accountable talk, where the goal is to encourage students to use language to communicate significantly, question critically, and make things happen.

Through the following events, which include telling jokes, making speeches, brainstorming, and interviewing, students can learn to speak with self-assurance, clarity, and a sense of the ideas and interests of the people with whom they are speaking. In a classroom focusing on accountable talk, there is an emphasis on active listening and connected inquiry and response. The strategies suggested provide students with opportunities to rehearse, practise, and develop listening and speaking skills for use both inside and outside the classroom. The contexts and events we have provided for oral communication demand thinking that calls on students to use imagination, analysis, and evidence-based opinion.

Joke and Riddle Telling: A Context for Talk Skills

Q: What's green and smells like purple paint?

A: Green paint!

Jokes and riddles demand to be read aloud. When you read a joke or riddle in a book or magazine that tickles your funny bone, you are often tempted to share it with others. Many jokes and riddles are written as question-and-answer dialogues. Knock Knock jokes always need one or more audience members to take part. Jokes and riddles can provide a lesson in communication.

Provide students with the following geography riddles and ask them to read them with a partner, one asking the questions, one giving the punch line. Have them repeat the activity, switching roles.

Who is the coldest relative on earth?	*Aunt Arctica.*
What's the coldest city in Germany?	*Brrrrr – lin.*
What happens when you throw a green rock in the Red Sea?	*It gets wet.*
What is purple and 50 000 kilometres long?	*The Grape Wall of China.*
Are the pyramids in Egypt?	*I sphinx so.*
Where do hamsters come from?	*Hamsterdam.*
Which city has the most eggs in the world?	*New Yolk City.*

Knock Knock!	Knock Knock!	Knock Knock!
Who's there?	*Who's there?*	*Who's there?*
Kenya.	Havana.	Jamaica.
Kenya who?	*Havana who?*	*Jamaica who?*
Kenya guess?	Havana great time on my vacation.	Jamaica mistake?

Ten Activities That Promote Talk Skills

The activities in this section are designed to have students read jokes or retell jokes to one or more friends. Each activity needs a speaker and listener(s). In this way, students have a context to enrich their talk skills—and laugh—as they communicate with others.

1. Students can make a comedy tape, reading aloud a variety of jokes and riddles for others to listen to. Let them work with friends. It is important for them to rehearse their routines before the tape recording to make sure that the punch line comes across clearly. They might choose a particular topic for the comedy tape (e.g., animal riddles, school jokes, or Knock Knock jokes).

2. Students can work in groups to rehearse and present a comedy show featuring favorite jokes and riddles. This show could be performed for others to watch or it could be videotaped.

3. Students can write four or five favorite jokes or riddles and survey others to find out which they think is the funniest of the selection. The data could be graphed. The class can create a top 10 list of jokes and riddles.

4. Create a bulletin-board display of jokes and riddles. One suggestion is to have the riddles displayed as if they were written on a graffiti wall.

5. Students can create an illustration of a favorite joke or riddle using dialogue balloons to show the conversation between characters.

6. The class can make a joke and riddle game by writing a number of jokes and riddles on file cards. The question part of the riddle can be put on one card and the answer on another (Q: What day do chickens hate the most? A: Fry-day). Students can then match question and answers.

7. Students can transform a favorite joke or riddle into a comic strip. Decisions need to be made about which characters to include, how dialogue will be written, and how the joke will be divided into three or four storyboard spaces.

8. Create a class anthology of jokes and riddles, with each student contributing at least one joke or riddle to the collection. These jokes and riddles could be compiled on the computer. The class might want to produce a published version through photocopying for others to read.

9. Students can write their own jokes or riddles. Many writers of jokes experiment with wordplay. Jokes with homonyms (sound-alike or almost sound-alike words), with homographs (words with more than one meaning), and with idioms are a good place to start.

10. Build a class collection of joke and riddle books, with students bringing in resources from home, school, or community library or ordering some from the book club. Have the class discuss which is the "best" joke book for students of their age to have.

Impromptu Speech Making

When someone is called to give an impromptu, or spur-of-the-moment, speech, that person might feel uneasy. Speaking in front of others is a fear that many people in the world have. If students are prepared, however, they can have what looks like an instant speech to meet any emergency speech situation.

The purpose of this activity is to encourage students to think on their feet, giving them confidence to meet impromptu situations. They can make impromptu speeches with a large group or with the whole class.

Each member of the group considers three topics that can be used for an instant speech. The topics should be of general interest to members of the class so that they can readily discuss them. Members record each of their three suggested topics on separate slips of paper and then put them into a box or a basket. Here are some suggestions:

pets	restaurants	doctors
books	dentists	brothers or sisters
superstitions	babysitting	vacations
barbecues	commercials	birthday parties
favorite foods	magazines	going on a picnic
taking pictures	camping	using the Internet
my favorite sport	games	fashion
nuclear weapons	global warming	recycling paper
having a curfew	dating	my neighborhood

One member of the group draws two slips of paper from the container, chooses one topic, and returns the other slip to the container. On a signal, the speaker must talk for exactly one minute, ending the speech when a signal or one-minute time card has been flashed by someone appointed to be the timer. The activity continues, until each group member has had a turn to present an instant speech.

Impromptu Speeches and English Language Learners

The focus of impromptu speeches is on listening and speaking, and the context is social and informal. These activities are not meant to be presentations or performances, but they do require students to speak out loud. English Language Learners can find this a bit daunting.

Although there is not a lot of pressure on the speakers, the talk is "accountable." The expectation is that both the listeners and the speakers will stay on task, listen respectfully to one another, learn something new about one another, expand their understanding about the topic under review, and have fun.

English Language Learners require a different kind of support to do this work. Probably the best idea is to have these students be the timers and the coaches so that they are still involved in the activity. Once they feel more comfortable and up to the challenge, they still will require encouragement and support from their peers as they make their impromptu speeches.

Extensions

1. Repeat the activity. The time limit is increased to two or three minutes.
2. The activity can be done as a circle game with three or four players. Each person chooses a topic to present. One person is chosen to be the timer, who calls "change" to give each person a turn to speak. On a signal, player 1 begins talking and when the timer calls "change," player 2 begins to speak. The game continues until each person has had three or four opportunities to speak. The speaker should offer new information about the topic rather than repeat information.
3. The game is played as a team, with each member discussing a topic that has been agreed upon by all. The conversation continues with each player, in turn, contributing to the speech for 30 seconds.
4. Each person can contribute an object that is concealed in a box or bag. The speaker chooses one, telling as much about it as possible.
5. Perhaps a picture of a person or place from a magazine, a scene on a postcard, a photograph, or an art print can be used. The teacher or group members can contribute items which are placed face down on a table. The activity is repeated with one person selecting an image on which to base an instant speech.

Under pressure, students might be tempted to talk fast, but the goal is to present information clearly and with confidence. Remind them that they need to speak slowly enough that listeners can take in their words.

Impromptu Speeches: Student Self-Assessment

The following questions can be used to help students consider their success at delivering an impromptu speech. Given the questions, students can write a "yes" or "no" answer to each. They can use the questions to prepare a self-assessment where they state what they did well and what they might improve upon. Alternatively, these questions can be raised in a one-to-one meeting with the students to consider their assessment of the learning that occurred.

- Is the purpose of the presentation is clear?
- Does it capture the audience's attention?
- Is the vocabulary descriptive and accurate?
- Is the audience engaged throughout the presentation?
- Did I choose language, examples, and visual aids that work together to heighten the audience's interest and connection to the topic?

Learning How to Question

"Ask a man to question and he inquires for a day; teach a man to question and he inquires for life."

—Dennis Palmer Wolf, "The Art of Questioning," in *Academic Connections* (Winter 1987)

Here's a question for students to discuss and answer with others: *When do we need to ask questions in our lives?*

When listening to others, we sometimes have a curiosity about what we are being told and find ourselves asking questions to help clarify ideas and better understand the topic at hand. When having conversations, interviewing others, or seeking information that others might know about, it is important to raise questions. Asking questions of a speaker, whether someone known or not yet met but from whom information is needed, helps the speaker to consider telling us what he or she knows. Sometimes, when listening to a report, questions wander in our heads, and we may pose questions after the speaker's presentation. In this way, we show that we are interested in what the speaker has to say and that we want to encourage a dialogue with the speaker or a discussion among those who listened to the speaker.

The following three activities will help students consider the range of questions they can ask about a topic, an idea, or a story.

1. Brainstorm questions for answers.

The television show *Jeopardy* demands that players ask questions to answers that are given in the game board. For this *Jeopardy*-like activity, students brainstorm a list of questions that can be asked for one of the answers listed below. As an example, "Newspaper" might prompt such questions as these: "Where did you see his picture?" "How did you wrap the fish?" "Who does the journalist work for?"

In the attic	My uncle	The clown
Alaska	The bank	Cats
Garbage	Ten	With glasses
Yellow	School	Money
"It's too hot!"	On the computer	"Terrific!"

Here are alternative ways to complete this activity:

- As a group, students give themselves a time limit. How many questions can they think of in that time?
- Students brainstorm 10 questions with a partner, recording their questions on a sheet of paper. When they have completed their list, partners compare it with another pair that has brainstormed questions for the same topic. As a group, students prepare a list of 25 to 30 questions.
- Students work with two or more classmates. Each player, in turn, provides a question to an agreed-upon topic. Continue the activity until no one can think of any more questions. This activity might be a competition so that the last person to think of a question is the winner.

2. Play the Witness Game.

This game will help students practise the art of asking and answering questions. Working with one or two classmates, they can choose one person to be the witness to an imaginary incident in the neighborhood (e.g., an accident, a theft, vandalism, an argument). The witness is being interviewed by a lawyer who has been called upon to investigate. The lawyer is to get as much detail from the witness as possible by asking questions. Students in role as lawyers will interrupt the witness at any time to ask for details that will add to the story being told.

> WITNESS: Last Friday I was walking along the street …
> LAWYER: What time of day was it?
> WITNESS: It was in the evening at about 7:30.
> LAWYER: Have you ever been down this street before?
> WITNESS: I was going to visit my friend who lives on Greensides Drive.
> LAWYER: Do you often go and visit your friend?

3. Audition to be a television talk-show host.

Students work in pairs. Tell students to imagine that they are applying for a job as a television talk-show host. To prepare for the job interview, they have been asked to brainstorm questions to ask famous people. As a challenge, students can brainstorm questions that they would ask a celebrity or historical figure no longer living (e.g., Elvis Presley, Mother Teresa, Mahatma Gandhi, Helen Keller, John F. Kennedy, Harriet Tubman, or Christopher Columbus). Provide 10 to 15 minutes for pairs to brainstorm questions.

Following the brainstorming, partners can be paired up to compare their questions. Which questions require only yes or no answers? Which question on the list is the most useful? Which is the most unimportant?

Extensions
1. The brainstorming activity can be repeated by having students work in groups of four. Students can brainstorm questions that they might ask a celebrity, a politician, a fictional character from a novel, or a nursery rhyme character.
2. Using the questions that have been prepared, students can present a talk-show interview. There can be more than one interviewer.

Interviewing: Conversation with a Purpose

One of the best ways to find out about someone, such as an author, celebrity, or politician, is to interview that person. In this way we can get first-hand information. An interview is an organized conversation with a purpose. Different kinds of interviews can be carried out, depending on the purpose of the interviewer. Students might wish to interview others to obtain information to be used in any of the following ways:

- **as a report:** Usually the person being interviewed is an expert on a particular topic.
- **as an argument:** The person being interviewed can be quoted as an authority on a particular topic. The statements obtained verify or back up an argument or debate that is being prepared.

- **as a profile:** The focus of this interview is to highlight the personality and life of a particular person. The person's work or hobbies may be discussed, but the main emphasis is on the person as an individual and how his or her character affects what the person does.

The success of an interview is often dependent on the types of questions asked. Most questions should be prepared in advance of the interview, although other questions may arise as students continue the conversation. It is important, too, to have a balance of direct and open-ended questions.

Direct Questions	**Open-Ended Questions**
These often require specific information from the interviewer. Answers are usually brief. *Examples:* Where did you go to elementary school? Do you have any pets? What book are you reading? How old were you when you became involved …? What was the hardest decision that you ever made?	These invite the opinions and views of the person being interviewed. Answers are generally longer and more detailed. *Examples:* How did you become interested in playing the drums? What is your opinion about downloading music from the Internet? How have the media affected your career? How has your success changed your life? If you could give your fans a piece of advice about pursuing their goals, what would it be?

Ten Interviewing Activities

One of the most striking aspects of caring classrooms is the fact that students are interested in one another—in their well-being, in their daily endeavors, in their dreams for the future. The students in caring classrooms know who is in the room. They are aware of each other's strengths and are thoughtful about the various challenges they face.

Interviewing activities provide a number of benefits to students. They allow students to work together to get to know each other better. They also encourage students to find out about others who are not part of the classroom environment but whose stories can contribute to a better understanding of the human condition. Interviewing activities encourage students to see that people have varying perspectives and often complex, layered stories to tell. While asking questions, students find out that people are somewhat the same and also very different from one another. They discover that all of us are in some way unique—and that it is important to acknowledge and be curious about the diversity of the human experience.

1. Brainstorm questions.

Students work in partners. Tell them to imagine that they are going to interview a famous author, sports figure, actor, or rock star. Together, they prepare a list of questions that they consider appropriate to ask the person chosen. Once they have prepared the list, prompt them to consider which questions are direct and which open-ended. They might write the questions in two columns under the headings "Direct" and "Open-Ended." When finished, have them join with another pair to compare and evaluate questions. In groups of four students then discuss these questions:

> Which questions would be the most effective? Why?
> Which questions do you think are the least important? Why?
> Is there a suitable balance of direct and open-ended questions?
> Which question do you think the interviewee would find the most interesting?

2. Interview in role on a nursery rhyme theme.

Students work in partners. Tell them to brainstorm a list of questions they might ask a nursery rhyme character. Partners conduct the interview with one person playing the nursery rhyme character and one person playing a reporter from a newspaper or magazine who has been asked to present an article on what happened to this character.

Example: A reporter asks questions to determine the true story of Jack and Jill, asked of Jill in the hospital emergency room.

> How old are you, Jill?
> Is Jack your twin brother?
> What were you doing going up the hill at that time of night?
> Did your brother make you accompany him?
> Were you not aware that the water in the well was poisoned and that the townspeople have not been allowed near that well for more than a month?
> Why did you disobey the Do Not Enter sign?

Students repeat the activity, but this time the person who played the story character will play the part of the reporter and the person being interviewed will be someone who might know something *about* the story character (e.g., a neighbor, an employer, a teacher, a relative).

Alternatively, to gain another perspective on the story, the role of reporter could be changed to that of an imaginary character with some logical relationship to the story. Students can brainstorm ideas about who the character should be and why that person's perspective would be of interest to the story. For example, the doctor who examined Jack and Jill could ask questions of the twins' mother to find out more about the two characters' well-being:

> Have the twins always been disobedient?
> Have they ever had a serious fall before?
> Do you think that punishment is necessary?
> What story did you hear from them?

3. Conduct an interview to prepare a report.

Have students plan an interview as part of a research project. A resource person in the specific subject area could be contacted. To help them practise their interviewing skills, suggest that students interview someone in their family or community about a specific job they have. Interviews could be tape-recorded to be used as part of the presentation of the project.

4. Interview classmates.

On a piece of paper, students write their names and three topics that interest them or that they are familiar with and could be interviewed about. In groups, or as a class, students pull each other's pieces of paper out of a box or basket. Once students have a piece of paper, they prepare to interview the person whose name they drew on one of the topics written down. When ready, they conduct the interview for 10 to 15 minutes. They can make notes that record the main points that have been shared. Alternatively, the interview can be recorded and transcribed later (see Activity 7). Students may wish to present the information learned to another pair or to the class.

5. Interview a character from a novel as a group.

Sometimes, interviews are conducted with more than one person asking the questions. In groups of three or four, students can choose a character from a novel they have read. One member of the group role-plays the novel character and the others role-play reporters, asking questions. Students should take turns so that each member of the group has a chance to role-play the character. They might role-play the same character or become another character from the same novel.

6. Collect published interviews.

Prompt students to collect samples of interviews that have appeared in magazines, newspapers, or books and share them with others. Ask these questions: "What information did you learn about this person from the interview? What question(s) do you find the most interesting? If you could continue the interview, what questions might you ask this person?"

7. Transcribe an interview.

After students have conducted an interview, suggest that they write it up as a transcript of the conversation. They can use notes taken during the interview, or if they have tape-recorded the interview, they can make a transcript of part of it by writing the exact words that each speaker has said. An interview is usually written in script form, with each speaker's conversation designated clearly.

8. Do a three-step interview.

In this interview strategy, group members interview one another on a particular topic. Partner 1 interviews partner 2. Partner 3 takes notes, recording key ideas from the given responses. The activity is repeated with roles being rotated so that all members of the group are interviewed.

Possible Interview Topics

Describe some memorable holidays or vacations you've had.

Tell about a time you hurt yourself or had an accident.

What qualities do you think are important for friendship?

Describe something that you think you are an expert at.

Describe the most memorable birthday party you've attended.

If you could enter a time machine, where would you travel to? Why?

9. Interview family members.

Sometimes the people most familiar to us are the best people to interview because they will provide honest opinions. Interviewing parents, relatives, or neighbors can help students gather information about a topic that can be reported back to class.

10. Provide tips for a good interview.

Ask students to imagine that a friend or older brother or sister is going for a job interview to work as a camp counsellor or to coach a team. In small groups, students can come up with advice on what to do when being interviewed. How should the person to be interviewed prepare? How should he or she present during the interview? How would an employer consider this person to be a successful interviewee?

Family-Related Topics
- What is your opinion of student homework?
- Who was your most memorable teacher? Why?
- What do you remember doing in your leisure time when you were younger?
- What were some of your favorite books when you went to school?

When Students Work in Groups: A Matter of Discussion

In a discussion, participants have a reason to speak: perhaps to analyze their feelings and responses, investigate solutions to a difficult human problem, or create something together that will make an artistic statement. Students can have a discussion with a partner, in small groups, or as part of a whole class.

It is important for students to share the leadership in groups—to take turns being the listener, the summarizer, the initiator, the supporter, the interpreter, the encourager, the tracker, the tension reliever, the scribe, and the reporter. The line master "Shared Leadership: Ten Group Roles to Practise" outlines the responsibilities associated with work in groups.

Discussion Skill Critiques

Have the students get into groups of five. Give each student two group discussion roles to play during a discussion about one of the following topics. A time limit of 20 minutes could be set.

- Marks are not necessary in school.
- How does society ignore the rights of children?
- Should the government allow homeless people to live on the streets?
- Should panhandlers be removed from the streets?
- Should daily physical education be made compulsory?
- The government should lower taxes on things that we buy.
- There should be tighter controls on television commercials and magazine advertisements.
- Weekends should be three days instead of two.
- Cell phones should be allowed in all classrooms.
- There should not be a dress code in school.
- There is too much violence on television and in films.
- The voting age should be lowered.
- The world does not need zoos.
- We shouldn't bother recycling our garbage.
- Does our society do enough for senior citizens?

Shared Leadership: Ten Group Roles to Practise

1. *The Initiator:* The participant begins the conversation in small groups by making a statement, asking a question, or giving an opinion.

2. *The Listener:* The participant listens attentively to what is being said and does not interrupt.

3. *The Supporter:* The participant supports differing opinions and encourages everyone to take part in the discussion.

4. *The Summarizer:* The participant takes time at a strategic moment in the discussion to summarize what everyone has said so far.

5. *The Tracker:* The participant helps people to get back on track when they stray into discussions that have nothing to do with the task at hand.

6. *The Interpreter:* The participant makes sure that the meaning of what is said is understood by the group.

7. *The Tension Reliever:* The participant breaks the tension by making people laugh and feel good about themselves.

8. *The Encourager:* The participant encourages everyone to contribute and to keep going.

9. *The Scribe:* The participant writes down salient points of the discussion.

10. *The Reporter:* The participant reports back to the group about what has been discussed or decided.

Pembroke Publishers © 2011 *Creating Caring Classrooms* by Kathleen Gould Lundy and Larry Swartz ISBN 978-1-55138-270-8

After students have finished their discussions, invite them to use the guidelines on the line master "Shared Leadership: Ten Group Roles to Practise" to talk about how effective they were in their various roles.

Extensions

1. Students organize in the same groups as the above activity, and discuss the same (or a different) topic for 15 to 20 minutes. This time they each take on a different role. For example if someone was an *avoider* last time, that person might take on the role of the *organizer* this time.

2. In groups of four, students develop a discussion guide where they list qualities of a good discussion. They consider what can be done to encourage group members who hinder a discussion to become more positive.

3. Students repeat the activity, either staying with the same group and choosing another topic, or organizing themselves into other groups. A longer time limit of 30 minutes could be set for the discussion.

4. Using the tape recording of another group discussion, a group can apply the guidelines to evaluate the effectiveness of the recorded discussion.

5. Each group in the class can decide upon one topic to discuss. At the end of the discussion, the leader or scribe could summarize the group discussion. As a class, the discussion can continue so that other points of view are heard.

Variation: In groups of 8 to 10, students can have a discussion on one of the topics listed above or on another topic that you have chosen for them to discuss. Before beginning, each student can take on one of the group discussion roles. Students either choose their own roles or put different role names on a piece of paper, with each person choosing one from a pile. Encourage the students to play that role throughout the discussion.

How SMART Boards Create Community

by Patrick Molicard Chartier

Patrick is a graduate of the Initial Teacher Education program at Ontario Institute for Studies in Education, University of Toronto, where he won an award of commendation for his excellent contributions. Patrick has taught Early Childhood Education courses at Humber College and taught at a sports camp in Switzerland. As an educational consultant, he helped to create a kindergarten school in a village in Ghana.

In today's classrooms, the use of SMART Boards is becoming more frequent, and there are many new factors this piece of technology brings to the classroom. Not only does the SMART Board enhance visual learning or add a new dimension to working with technology, but it can create a new sense of community among all who gather around to share, to explore, to inquire.

As a teacher candidate in the Initial Teacher Education program, I had the opportunity to use a SMART Board throughout my placement at an inner-city school. At first, it seemed that I was using the device in the same way as I would use a white board or chalkboard. The response from the students was neither more nor less engaged than my other teaching experiences.

On a Trip Together

I decided to use the SMART Board in a different way, to provide a more dynamic approach for the students to raise their own questions, make connections to the material, and take a more critical approach to that material. The SMART Board, I realized, wasn't just for me, but needed to involve the students working together with me and with one another.

For a math lesson where I planned to introduce linear measurement, I decided to draw on a significant event that had been in the news: the rescue of Chilean miners. The students were fascinated by the story. I attempted to illustrate what 700 metres looked like. The SMART Board helped to hook the students into understanding the far-below-ground reality and threat that the miners faced. I used Google Earth (free software) to show where we are in the world and where Chile is—an interactive way to see how far apart we are. Once we were looking at Chile, I zoomed in on where the mine was located. From that point, I carried on with my lesson. Little did I know how much this brought us all together. Through technology, all of us were able to go on a trip at the same time.

The success of this lesson spurred me on to consider other potential uses of the SMART Board, this time with a Social Studies lesson.

Globe-Trotting via Technology

I asked the students to share where they and their families came from. By typing the data into the program, we could see the globe move from exactly where we were located in Toronto to where the students came from. It gave us a concrete, visual representation of the distance many of the students travelled to be here as well as the diversity of areas. It had many pictures posted by travellers of the respective areas we visited.

The students eventually created passports. Over the course of my practicum placement, the class used the Internet to make virtual visits to various parts of the world. This activity was a meaningful way to further appreciate our diversity as a class and bring more understanding to our differences and similarities. The SMART Board allowed us to see and understand our individual histories in an engaging and relevant way.

From my experience, I came to understand that if the SMART Board is used just for the sake of using technology, then it will not enhance the lesson. If, however, it is used in a manner in which other media such as chalkboards and white boards cannot be used, it will change something in the classroom. It will build communication and collaboration as students gather around to learn with and from it, the teacher, and one another.

An Online Social Network: Real People in Real Situations

by Lisa Donohue

Lisa is an educator and author based in York Region, Ontario. As a literacy champion, she has worked with teachers across the province to find creative solutions and innovative teaching techniques in order to develop balanced literacy programs. She is the author of several books for teachers, including The Write Voice *and* Independent Reading Inside the Box.

As an educator, I find that my Professional Learning Network (PLN) is one of my most powerful resources. This network consists of colleagues I trust and admire, people whose opinion I value and whose advice I respect. We share our challenges and our successes, provide suggestions and resources, and discuss our different teaching strategies. We celebrate when things go well, and we provide consolation and re-direction when they don't go as we had planned. These colleagues are a part of my daily life. Their presence lets me know that I am not alone in my journey of teaching and learning.

My PLN is made up of the colleagues I know face-to-face, but is also composed of a plethora of people I know only through online learning communities. An online social network is a place to meet others, share ideas, and engage in rich dialogues with professionals around the world. Venues such as Twitter and blogs have provided countless opportunities for educators to connect, collaborate, and communicate about important issues facing learners today. With a few clicks of a keyboard, it is possible to share an important idea, ask a question, or discover a new and innovative resource.

Helping Students Plug In to Communicate

Is it possible to bring the power of an online learning community into our classrooms? Students in the 21st century consider online communications an extension of face-to-face conversations; they easily alternate between these various forums. They are often referred to as *digital natives* because they have been brought up in a world surrounded by the latest technology. Although these students may be more familiar with technological devices, they may not know how to use them responsibly and understand the complexities that exist when communicating in an online environment. As educators, we can help our students harness the power of these social networking tools and assist them in developing the skills they need in order to actively contribute as digital citizens.

Four classes interacting through Edmodo

In a unique initiative, students in four separate classes in different schools were connected to form a micro-online community. Through the establishment of this student PLN, we introduced students to the social norms affiliated with working in an online community. We wanted them to discover the power of working collaboratively with other students they did not know face-to-face, we wanted to foster a positive learning climate through mutual respect and trust, and we wanted them to begin to share, create, and communicate in an online community.

The students were connected through the Web 2.0 tool Edmodo (www.edmodo.com), a social network created explicitly for educators. Edmodo appears and functions in a manner similar to Facebook. A secure site, it requires all students to have an access key in order to log on, and teachers maintain full administrative privilege—they can review, edit, or delete posts as necessary. In this manner, students are free to interact in an online community that is secure and protected from unwanted visitors.

Dialoguing about learning skills

Three other teachers in different schools and I began to introduce our students to the power of social networking. Students, from different geographical locations, ranged from Grades 4 to 8. Initially, we wanted students to begin to understand that the members of this online community were real people with real feelings and real experiences. Students were placed into one of six subgroups. They began by introducing themselves and sharing their interests. Each subgroup was then assigned a different learning skill (e.g., Independent Work, Responsibility, Initiative, Collaboration, Organization, or Self-Regulation). Working with their online community, students began posting personal definitions of these skills, as well as commenting on the posts of others. They were able to use Edmodo as a vehicle through which to have a dialogue about their ideas. Students posted their definitions and commented on the posts of others. As they dug deeper into their personal definitions for the learning skills, they were able to share ideas, re-think their own opinions, and provide feedback to others.

Once students had developed a deeper understanding of the definitions of the various learning skills, they used any media tool of their choice (e.g., www.animoto.com, www.bitstrips.com, www.glogster.com, www.voicethread.com, www.bighugelabs.com, or www.prezi.com) to create a promotional piece that would share the importance of a specific learning skill. Students created an initial draft of their media piece and posted it to their social network.

Giving and receiving feedback

Having built an online community of respect and trust, students provided feedback to one another regarding their work. Students were encouraged to post their observations and questions, rather than their criticisms and suggestions. The students were then able to re-think and revise their media piece, based on the feedback of others in their online social network. Finally, the project culminated with all of the separate media presentations being combined through a VoiceThread. This final media piece was posted on Edmodo to be shared with all of the students.

As students began to interact more with one another through this online forum, a great deal of their learning took place informally. While we had set the stage for them to interact with one another and established the tasks for them, the power of the social network began to take on a life of its own. In one instance, one of my students had encountered a digital tool used by someone else in his online learning group. He was fascinated with this unique animation tool (www.xtranormal.com) and couldn't wait to get home to "try it out." As he entered the school the next day, he was bursting to share this new digital tool with me and the rest of the class. His "discovery" was only possible because of his interaction with the online community.

A Valuable Lesson on How to Interact

One of the most valuable learning experiences happened incidentally and yet served as a powerful source of dialogue for my students. As students were posting feedback to their group, a student (let's call her Sara) posted a comment that was highly critical. While it did not contain content that was offensive, the tone did not demonstrate respect. Sara had reviewed Jared's media presentation and wrote feedback that described the project as "boring." By the time I discovered the comment, it was too late to delete it. Jared had already posted a response, and it was clear that his feelings had been hurt. While Sara did not intend to be hurtful, she could not "take back" the post. Although it was possible to delete the post, damage had clearly already been done. Jared's feelings were hurt, and the only way to move forward was to respond with an apology. Although this incident was only a minor hiccup in the feedback process, it was a valuable lesson to all students that once something is posted on the Internet, there is no way to know how many other people have accessed it and it is not always possible to "take it back."

While this micro-online community did not function as a full-fledged PLN might, through the Edmodo project, students began to understand that their learning community is broader than their classroom. The students discovered the value of learning collaboratively through online tools. They were eager to try new tools that they saw others using and eager to seek input from their social network. They realized that an online social network is made up of real people with real feelings. They learned that they should always interact with others in a caring manner, whether they are meeting face-to-face or online. They learned that online conversations are just as real and powerful as face-to-face ones and that they should always be careful of what they post on the Internet. They learned that learning partners are available through digital tools and that an online learning community broadens the number of people they can share with and seek input from. Through this project, the students came to a deeper understanding of the learning skills. They were able to think of practical ways in which they could show these skills in everyday learning, and provided and applied feedback and input from their online community. Moreover, they learned the importance of using a PLN and the power of social networking; they also developed positive online etiquette—all in a secure, online learning environment.

Chapter 3

Building Collaboration

Collaboration requires individuals to embrace the potential confrontation of existing assumptions of expectations, a willingness "not to know" and to trust the people, and furthermore the process. One must have the ability to take risks, make a commitment to and take responsibility for the process. One must also maintain artistic integrity, embrace a balance of confidence and humility, be honest, be flexible, and willing to accept rejection or modification of personal ideas. One must be prepared to accept potential failure, tolerate discomfort, and conflict and live with— not against—difference. In short one must have a true desire to embrace complexity.

—From *Across Oceans: Writings on Collaboration* by Maxine Heppner (p. 44)

We are both fortunate to be able to visit a number of classrooms in our role as consultants and university instructors. It is easy to recognize a classroom community where students feel comfortable working with each other. There is an air of comfort as the students work together; there is a sea of authentic conversations and a buzz of joyful learning. The arrangement of desks, the stance of the teacher, and the opportunities for active, collaborative experiences are some indicators.

Talking Together, Working Together, Learning Together

A teacher candidate relayed the following story after her first practicum visit. On a visit to a Grade 5 classroom, the teacher candidate noticed a large open space at the back of the classroom. Curious how this was used from day to day, she asked the teacher. The reply: "Oh, we never use that space because the kids just can't seem to work well together." The teacher candidate felt that she should have spoken up because she wondered, *How will they ever learn to work together if they aren't given occasions to do so? When will the students learn to experience the pleasure of working with others as well as the frustrations that often need to be overcome to ensure success and the pleasure of collaborating?*

David and Roger Johnson, authors of *Learning Together and Learning Alone: Cooperative, Competitive and Individualistic Learning*, remind us that life is filled with groups from the moment of birth to the moment of death. As humans we have an inherent social nature. We learn, work, worship, and play in groups.

Many children first encounter group conversation in small, informal family interactions that may arise during mealtime or at parties or other occasions when relatives or family and friends gather together. Within our family and peer groups we are socialized into ways of behaving and thinking. As individuals grow and experience wider social contexts, greater discussion skills are demanded.

In the classroom, the context of small-group discussion provides a meaningful social dynamic for collaborative learning, where interaction, negotiation, and communication can develop effectively. The focus must be on the learning that grows from the talking and thinking that emerge as students make decisions, solve problems, question, argue, create, and plan together.

Group talk is concerned with getting things done, exploring, questioning, and arriving at conclusions no one person could have reached alone. In this forum, students can clarify and modify their ideas. As participants build on the talk of others to carry discussion forward, the skills promoted through interaction have the potential for social and language growth. Being successful in group discussion requires using both knowledge of the topic—though knowledge of a topic is not all that necessary to discuss it effectively—and of social situations to determine what to say, how to say it, when to say it, to whom to address it—and when not to say anything!

To be successful in group discussion, an individual must know how to operate in ways that are appropriate for the particular social context, which includes the setting, the physical arrangement of group members, the focus topic, the assigned task, the allotted time, and the members' roles. The context also includes many less clearly defined factors: the individual perspectives and expectations of each member, interpersonal relationships among participants, and the mutual expectations of all group members. The context may change from moment to moment, as different members speak, or as the understanding of the task changes. As the context changes, role relationships and behaviors also change. When group talk functions effectively, the students can experiment with the roles of leader and participant at different times. Being aware of the context, defining it, matching one's behavior to it, and signalling out loud thoughts to others are important group discussion skills.

Meaningful conversations will occur among students and teachers if contexts are such that students feel that their ideas are respected and valued by teachers and peers. A teacher who puts groups of students to work on some problem or task sends the important message to students that developing their own thoughts, and not just someone else's, is significant.

According to Gordon Wells, author of *The Meaning Makers*, teachers who invite students to contribute to discussions rather than simply telling or giving them answers demonstrate that "knowledge is jointly constructed in the collaborative meaning-making that occurs as people attempt to solve particular problems."

Ten Ways to Form Groups

1. Allowing the students to sort themselves into groups is perhaps an easy way to form groups. However, consideration needs to be made for students who always choose to work with the same people and often some students are uncomfortable fitting themselves into a group.

2. Students are randomly numbered off (e.g., 1-2-3). Once students have been assigned numbers, have them stand or raise their hands to find out who is in the same group.

3. Provide colored sheets or file cards. Groups can be arranged by having students meet with those who have the same color or by finding others who have a different color.

4. Determine groups in advance by considering a balance of abilities, genders, leadership capacity, language facility, interests, and social skills.

Kinds of Groups

- *Social:* Students choose who they work with.
- *Interest:* Students work together based on topic interest.
- *Gender:* There is a balance of males and females.
- *Ability:* Groups are formed by ability.
- *Homogeneous:* Members are similar in ability.
- *Heterogeneous:* Members are mixed in ability.
- *Teacher-assigned:* Groups are determined based on a relevant criterion.

5. Students are arranged in a circle or in a line (e.g., alphabetically, by birthday). Students then form groups by numbering off, for example, counting 1-2-3-4-5 to form groups of five.

6. Consider gender balance. In many classrooms, particularly with older grades, students feel comfortable working with peers of the same gender. Developmentally, many boys choose to work with boys and girls with girls. At times, groups can be single gender, but when groups are randomly made, attention can be paid to mixing up boys and girls.

7. Assign by interest groups. For example, introduce novels for students to read and after listening to your recommendations, students choose a novel that interests them. Interest groups can also be formed for research topics (e.g., animals) where students join together to gather and present information on something that interests them.

8. Use a random method. Students choose a card from a deck of cards and meet together with those who have the same suit. Or, students choose a manipulative block, a lollipop, or a sticker. They meet in groups with those who have the same item as they do.

9. Play an active game, such as Face to Face or Line Tag. When the game draws to a conclusion, explain to students that they will now be working with the person who is next to them, facing them, or behind them.

10. Invite the students to consider the best way to form groups for an activity.

Games That Build Collaboration

Collaboration requires a certain generosity of spirit, patience, maturity, listening skills, and a definite "buy in" to the classroom work by all involved. In fact, most students usually have no difficulty collaborating with others as long as the work has some sort of personal connection to them and if their voice and ideas are heard by all. Teachers need to ensure that those who are shy or learning English as a second language have an opportunity to offer their ideas. It is important to be aware of whose voices are present a lot of the time and whose voices are often silent. Everyone in the group needs to become aware of who is in the room so that there is a more inclusive ethic about the work that lies ahead.

All voices—even the ones that ask difficult questions or are unsure about the merits of some of the ideas being put forward—need to be heard. Making sure that all ideas are heard takes more time but often what students create together is of much better quality.

Part of the work of the collaborative classroom focuses on having students imagining, inventing, and creating something together. It means that students are talking with one another in partners, in small groups, and as a whole class to examine and debate different perspectives about material that matters. As they engage in collaborative talk and work alongside each other in collaborative activities, students become more knowledgeable about the content and also begin to see that their particular classroom community is made up of people who think differently and respond in many unique ways. This knowledge of difference, this understanding of varied response, this experience of having to open oneself up to something that one has never thought of before, allows students to become more empathetic to differing viewpoints, perspectives, and reactions. The classroom may be noisier, the work may be more intense, but it is also more interesting because it is more alive with people who want to share their ideas rather than worrying that they might be wrong. A collaborative classroom encourages debate, interaction, thoughtfulness, problem solving, and ambiguous response.

Untangle

This drama game provides an instant challenge for students to work together to solve a problem. Students are divided into groups of 8 to 10, and each group forms a circle, members standing. Direct students to stretch out their arms to the front of their bodies. Each student takes the hand of another student, connecting with two different students. On a signal, challenge the students to untie the knot of tangled hands—no one can let go of a partner's hands. The students are successful if they can return to a circle formation.

Extensions

1. Repeat the activity, but this time, students are not allowed to talk.
2. Have an Untangle competition. Which group can untangle in the quickest time?
3. Increase the group size to 12 or more to form a tangle. Are the students able to untangle as efficiently as they did in smaller groups?

Name Call, Ball Toss

Students stand in a circle. To begin, a ball is given to one player, who calls his or her name and tosses the ball to someone else in the circle. The ball continues to be passed, ensuring that all become familiar with the names in the group. The activity is repeated. This time, students start with their hands folded in front of them; after tossing the ball to someone else in the circle, they place their hands behind their backs. In this way, each person passes (and receives) the ball once. The activity is repeated again, following the sequence of passing the ball. Draw the students' attention to the pattern that has been established.

Extensions

1. Challenge the students to complete the activity within a certain time.
2. Students pass the ball in the same pattern without calling names.
3. The pattern of passing the ball is reversed. The ball is passed from the last person to the first person.
4. Two balls are passed, one using the original pattern and one using the reverse pattern.
5. Students find a new spot in the circle. The game is repeated.
6. Additional balls, up to five, are added.

Word Call

Students now choose a word or phrase that has been placed in an envelope. These words can be on a particular topic (e.g., food) from a script or from a novel. The words listed below are from the novel *Hatchet* by Gary Paulsen.

TURBULENCE	MICROPHONE
HELP	DIFFICULTY
CPR	OVER
PLEASE …	SIGNAL BREAKING UP

DOWN-ANGLE	HOPELESS STATIC
STILL TREMBLING	EASY SAY
INCREASED SPEED	HARD DO
HORIZON	REDUCE THE IMPACT
TRANSMITTER	WINDMILLING PROPELLER
EMPTY AIR WAVES	COCKPIT
HELLO?	PLANE DOWN
SOUND OF HIS OWN SOBS	

Explain to the students that the word they have selected will be their word or phrase—they need to "own" it. Tell them that they need to remember their word or phrase.

Students stand in a circle to play the game. This time when someone tosses the ball to someone in the circle, the word or phrase they own is called out. The game continues until everyone has had a chance to receive the ball and throw it. Like the Name Call, Ball Toss exercise, the students need to pay attention to who throws and receives the ball.

The activity is repeated, but students are asked to add an emotional dimension to the word or phrase. So, as they throw the ball and say the word, they need to do it perhaps angrily, sweetly, with despair. Ask the students: "How does the meaning of the word or phrase change? What images come to mind?"

Extension

Students work in groups of three to five to create a short scene in which everyone says their word. What order will they present the words? What physical gesture will they add as they say the line? Who is the line being said to? Provide students with time to rehearse their short scenes before sharing them with the whole class.

Variation: This exercise could be adapted to make it about the students' own identities. Have the students come up with a word that describes them. (These words could be alliterative, for example, Marvellous Martha, Energetic Ed.) The game is repeated with students calling out adjectives. Conclude by asking the following questions:

- What is our collective identity in the classroom?
- What do these words say about us as a group of people?
- What questions do you have about some of the words that were chosen?
- How can we reflect on these words to learn new things about ourselves as a community of learners?

Photo Contest

With thanks to Debbie Nyman

Students are divided into three groups (or four if there is a large number). To begin each group can decide on a name for their team. One team is invited to sit down while the other two groups are told that they are going to create a photo. The judges can have their backs turned to the players, and on a signal they are invited to turn around to declare which of the two groups is going to be the "winner" of the photo contest.

A caption is provided and group members are given 60 seconds to spontaneously create the corresponding photo as a still image to show the judges. Once the images are made, judges turn around and examine the two photos. The group discusses which of the pictures should get the prize. Encourage the judges to give

Possible Caption Titles

Halloween Night

The Parade

Haunted House

The Weekend

Off to War

reasons for their choices. What criteria are they using to judge the success of the photo?

The game is replayed with the judges replacing the group that won; a new photo caption is given.

Playful Lessons That Foster Collaborative Thinking

The lessons that follow offer opportunities for students to work together collaboratively over a period of time. The sources and strategies involve students in working beyond games to share ideas, solve problems, and learn to cooperate with one another. Students work in pairs or in small groups.

Creating a Monster: A Challenge in Collaboration

The following is an exercise in creativity as well as in non-verbal communication. To prepare for this collaborative activity, a variety of materials should be assembled in an envelope or box (e.g., feathers, pipe cleaners, straws, paper clips, elastics, tinfoil, and cardboard strips). Each kit could contain the same materials, or supplies could be placed randomly so that each group receives a different variety of items.

To launch the exploration, the teacher reads aloud "The Grebigol" or makes the students copies of the line master (next page).

1. The class is divided into groups of three or four. Students sit in a circle at a table or on the floor. A kit is given to each group. Direct the students not to open the package until a signal is given to do so.

2. Explain to the class that each group is going to work together to produce a single Grebigol creature, using any of the materials from the kit.

3. Explain to the class that, until the activity is completed, no one may talk. Students may neither speak nor pass notes to one another.

4. On a signal, students are invited to complete the sculpture. The sculptures can be put on display for other groups to use.

It is important for each group to discuss how it felt to assemble the Grebigol together, especially without talking. The self-assessment profile can be used at this time to help students reflect on their involvement in the project and on how successfully they worked to complete the project collaboratively. (See page 91.)

Alternatively, students could create a dragon, a bird, a forest or sea creature, or an alien being.

Creating the Grebigol: Teaching Tips

- Challenge the students to use all the materials in the envelope.
- Approximately 20 to 25 minutes is suggested for this activity, but explain to the students that they don't need to rush to complete the creature. As the activity unfolds, observe whether the majority of students need more time or whether it can be drawn to a closure.
- One challenge is to ask students to create a free-standing creature, one that won't easily fall apart. In this way the finished sculptures can be put on display or used for further writing or drama exploration.

The Grebigol

Winter has left its mark upon the land. The hills and valleys are empty, desolate, and stark. Nothing moves. The trees are blue and black against the frozen earth. Everything is waiting for spring.

Slowly, slowly, as the earth tilts back upon its axis, warmth is coming to the icy world. The snow is beginning to melt away, the rivers are catching the snow as it melts and begins its journey to the sea. Fresh, tender grass is beginning to break through the sunlight. The forest is beginning to come to life.

Somewhere high in those mountains is a long forgotten valley—a peaceful and beautiful valley. The north stirs and begins to rumble. Is it an earthquake? The chipmunks stop dead in their tracks. The birds cease their singing. The earth buckles up, cracks, and crumbles and begins to fall away. Something is coming up out of the earth, out of the depths of the den where he has slept away the long cold winter. It is the giant GREBIGOL.

The GREBIGOL is hungry. He hasn't eaten all winter. He begins to eat the new fresh grass. He reaches down and gobbles up new saplings, berries, and bushes. He is devouring the chipmunks, the birds, and the foxes. As he eats, he is heading down the canyon.

As he nears the town, he begins to eat telephone poles. He eats a dog and a cat. He swallows two garbage cans, a gas station, and a policeman. Now he is eating a new Volkswagen. He eats everything in sight … eating, crunching, munching, and gobbling until finally he is satisfied. Full, he cannot eat any more.

His eyelids are getting heavy. He is stuffed and getting very tired. Slowly, painfully, he begins to pull himself back up into the mountains, back to his den where he will dig his way back down into the earth. He will sleep there for another year until he is hungry again!

Author unknown

Pembroke Publishers © 2011 *Creating Caring Classrooms* by Kathleen Gould Lundy and Larry Swartz   ISBN 978-1-55138-270-8

Encourage the students to reflect on how successfully they worked in the group to prepare and present this work. How was this activity similar to or different than the silent collaborative activity of creating the creature?

Extension

Students work in small groups to create a short poem to accompany the creation. Poems, written on small file cards, can be used to describe the creature or give information or narrative about the Grebigol. Once groups have written poems, they could prepare a choral reading. Members decide how each line could be read, how lines of text could be divided, what sounds could be included, and what movements or physical formations could be used to present the poem to others in the class.

Tic Tac Tale: Group Story Making

A chart such as the line master meant especially for use by younger students (next page) is given to the students, who work in groups of three or four. The students are told to select any three items that appear in a row (as if they were playing Tic Tac Toe). Once the group has decided which row to work on, members improvise a story that includes those three items in some way.

Extensions

The following activities are alternative strategies for using the Tic Tac Tale chart in a variety of group situations.

1. Choose two rows to build a story.
2. Act out the story that has been invented.
3. Present the story in mime only or as a dance drama.
4. Each student in the group adds one sentence to build a continuous story; the group has three minutes to complete the story.
5. Students make a chart with new phrases (e.g., toad, prince, castle).
6. Students use their invented stories as stimuli for writing original tales.

Variation: The following version of the Tic Tac Tale chart can be presented to middle-years students and beyond:

A pop star	A stolen car	A deserted parking lot
A charm bracelet	A text message	A deadline
An empty street	A locked box	A baseball hat

Admirable Qualities: A Ranking

Character education relies on a culture of inclusiveness, equity, and a respect for diversity. It is dependent on the kinds of community that exist in our classrooms where students develop self-discipline and interpersonal skills and understand that it is important to do the right thing even when doing so is difficult.

The list that appears on page 76 is written on a chart or the chalkboard, or distributed as a handout.

Tic Tac Tale

Work with some friends. Choose three squares in a row. Together, use the items to develop a story.

A lonely princess	A unicorn horn	A dark forest
A rusty coin	A golden wand	A treasure map
An empty fountain	An ancient scroll	A small cottage

Pembroke Publishers © 2011 *Creating Caring Classrooms* by Kathleen Gould Lundy and Larry Swartz   ISBN 978-1-55138-270-8

- honesty
- reliability
- good listening skills
- strength
- generosity
- intelligence
- risk-taking
- sense of humor
- helpfulness
- work ethic
- resourcefulness
- creativity

Working independently, students consider how important each quality is to being successful in life and then rank the items in order of importance, starting with the most important.

Students then work in groups and share their individual ranking of qualities. A discussion should take place to reach a consensus.

The whole class can discuss the items with the goal of finding a ranking order for the qualities which everyone agrees to.

Variation #1: Ask students these questions: "How might this ranking list change if you were the head of a hospital wanting to hire a new nurse? the chairperson of a day-care board of directors wanting to hire a supervisor? the manager of a construction company who needs to hire a plumber?"

Variation #2: Students work in groups to brainstorm qualities associated with one of the following topics: a successful holiday, a restaurant they would like to eat at, a fun birthday party, a new computer, a television program worth watching, a new teacher they would want to hire, a babysitter, a new city mayor they would want to vote for. Groups can exchange lists and rank the qualities in order.

An Ideal Creation: Designing Together

Tell the students to imagine that the classroom is absolutely empty. It has no furniture, no people, no equipment. Working in groups of three or four, students can create their ideal classroom, suggesting how to refurnish the space. Students should draw their plans on a large sheet of chart paper. Once completed, each group can report to the large group, describing its designs for the ideal classroom.

Variations: Students might work in groups to create other designs, such as for a new neighborhood park, a playground for young children, a shopping mall, a restaurant, or a home on an alien planet.

Word Web Spin: Brainstorm

Students work with one or two classmates. Each group is given a different topic word. The challenge is for the students to brainstorm as many words associated with that word as they can. To begin, create a sample on the board or on a chart to demonstrate how to display the word web. For instance, students might suggest words associated with the word *green*.

Variation: Once the students have created their word webs, encourage them to add to them by brainstorming more words that can grow out of the original words placed on their web.

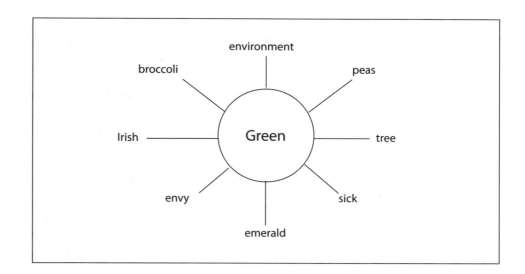

Possible Word Web Words

Bully

Friendship

Peace

Tests

Red

Hospitals

Emotions

Packing for the Moon: Making Hard Choices

This activity offers students a context for giving and receiving ideas and collaborating to solve a particular problem. Provide students with the following list of items.

cell phone	compass
change of clothes	first aid kit
statistics: (e.g., climate and population of various countries)	diamonds and gold
	food and water
diary or log book	watch
oxygen mask	tape recorder
personal computer	digital camera
newspaper	video camera
matches	personal identification
GPS	pocket mirror

Alternatively, hand out blank index cards and choose any 10 to 12 of the items from the above list for the students to record.

Tell the students: "Let's imagine that you have been given an opportunity to travel to the moon. Take a look at your list and circle the three items that you would most want to have with you if you were to travel into the future today." Students should understand that each person can carry one knapsack of personal items—all supplies, food, medicines, and other necessities will be available on the mission. An experienced astronaut will guide them to ensure their safety.

To begin, students work individually, to prepare their list of what they will take in a knapsack. A time limit of five minutes is given for individuals to complete their list to share with others who are going on the journey. Once the lists are completed, students meet in groups of four or five to share them.

Extension

Tell students that there has been a change of plan. Only one knapsack per group will be allowed on the spaceship. Each knapsack can take only two items. Students then review their list as a group. Now they have to work together to reach a consensus about those two items. This challenge might take a while. Allow the conversations to continue for five minutes or so, but then stop the discussions to hear how the process is going. Students often have strong opinions about what to take and what could be left behind. Encourage them to really listen to one another as they find ways of negotiating their choices. Have them consider the cramped space on the spacecraft, the conditions on the moon, the viability of taking perishables, and so on. This is a great exercise to promote oral language through brainstorming, discussion, and negotiation.

101 Things About "The Beast": Making Lists

Security is something that has affected the way that we travel and the way that famous people conduct their lives.

List 1: Have students talk about the kinds of security measures that are now in place in all airports around the world. Have them create a list of the procedures that most travellers follow from the moment they enter an airport to the time that they arrive at their desired destination. Have students compare lists.

List 2: Present the image of the Beast, U.S. President Obama's 2008 Cadillac which carries him around the country and in other countries. Students work in groups to brainstorm all of the features found on the outside of Obama's car.

List 3: Students work in the same groups to create a list of all of the features found in the inside.

Extension
Have students compare their lists with these details found on the Internet: military-grade body at least five-inches (12 cm) thick, pump-action shotguns and tear-gas cannons, bottles of the president's blood in case transfusion needed, oxygen and firefighting system in trunk, reinforced steel under car to protect against bombs, tires reinforced with Kevlar, and armour-plated doors eight inches (20 cm) thick. Ask students what items surprised them. What questions do they have about this car? What further research could they do to create another kind of list?

Poem Puzzles

Three related activities follow.

• *Putting the Poem in Order*
Students work together in groups of three or four to solve a puzzle. As they discuss the poem, they can argue, negotiate, question, describe, and explain what they think the poem is about. Short, unrhymed poems of about 15 lines are most suitable. Students are provided with lines of a poem that have been taken out of order. In pairs or small groups, students work to put the lines into an order that they think makes best sense. When each pair has reorganized the poem, they can share their version with another pair. You could conclude the activity by sharing the original version of the poem with the class.

• *Comparing Unjumblings*
Each line of a poem is written on a separate strip of paper. Students are given an envelope with a number of strips. The challenge is to arrange the lines in a way that they think is most suitable. They can, if they wish, cut their strips and make more lines to cut a poem. When the group is satisfied with their final version, they can glue the poem onto a piece of construction paper. Groups can compare the different ways they presented their poems. As part of the discussion, encour-

Sample Poem for Poem Puzzles

We have tomorrow.
Bright before us
Like a flame.

Yesterday
A night-gone thing,
A sun-down name.

And dawn today
Broad arch above the road we came.
We march!

Langston Hughes

age students to explain their reasons for arranging the poem as they did. Share the original version of the poem with the students. Have them discuss how the meaning of the poem changes by the way the lines are organized.

• *From Prose to Free-Verse Poem*

This activity fulfills the goal of seeing how words can be arranged freely, sometimes resulting in a poem. Display the lines of a short poem written in prose form, that is, one continuous sentence without line breaks. Students can work in pairs or in groups of three to shape the words into a poem. They divide the lines in free-verse style, using varied line lengths, white spaces, and indentations.

To build on the activity, students can choose one or two lines from a novel or information text they are reading. They transform these words into a free-verse poem by rearranging the words in a varied order. Encourage students to eliminate, repeat, or perhaps add some words that they think would work towards creating a poem.

A line master students can use to assess their group participation appears on page 91.

"Minute Book," the poem below, illustrates how even one sentence can be treated like a free-verse poem.

I will give each hour
A name
So that, when I'm dying
I will look at them again,
Point to some and smile
"that hour was my friend."

Julie O'Callaghan

Introducing Collaborative Literacy Events

The kinds of collaborative literacy events that we describe here are designed to make all students feel that they are connected to learning about and in language. In these lessons and activities, students discover the power of language as they play with it. They find their authentic voices as they tell us a little about themselves, as they connect their personal lives to the texts that they are working with, and as they talk themselves into understanding. As they work together, negotiating and sharing meaning, they are experimenting with language and thinking in new ways. They assimilate ideas that are new to them, learn new vocabulary, and explore compelling questions to which there are multiple answers. They are engaged in all kinds of different discussions, sharing personal stories and presenting new insights to others, either in small groups or to the whole class. As they gain confidence, they learn that there are many different ways to use language to solve problems. As they listen to one another, they gain new perspectives and learn to accommodate different points of view. Collaborative literacy events are part of a caring classroom because they encourage students to question what they are learning, allow varied responses, and encourage active, engaged group work where everyone is involved.

The collaborative literacy events that follow include problem solving, choral dramatization, literature circles, and writing experiences. They encompass both strategies and skills.

Problem-Solving Together

"Hey, why didn't I think of that!" Brainstorming helps us to share ideas with others, piggyback on ideas that others might have, and create a storm inside our heads to come up with ideas and thoughts around a certain topic.

Ask students to imagine that they are applying to work for a company called Brainstorm Inc. Those who work at the company are known for their skills at solving problems creatively and for their ability to work with others. For the job interview, the manager of the company has identified the following problems.

Students working with one or two classmates choose one of these challenges or questions, and brainstorm for three minutes only:

Challenges
- List things that are difficult.
- List things that are blue.
- List things that we read.
- Describe a monster.
- Invent some new pie flavors.

Questions
- How many ways can you use a toothpick?
- What are some words that are more than four syllables?
- What are some ways to recycle plastic bottles?
- How can we make schools better in the future?
- What would happen if the world did not have any numbers?

Brainstorming to Problem-Solve

1. Students work with one or more classmates. Together, the students choose one of the problems to solve and take turns providing a solution to the problem. How long might they continue to brainstorm the problem together?

2. Students work with a partner. Together, they choose a problem. They repeat the above activity, writing as many solutions as they can in three minutes. They then compare their list with their partner's to see which ideas are the most original.

3. Students work with a partner. Together, they choose another problem from the list to brainstorm. This time they can work together to write as many solutions as they can to the problem. No time limit applies. They then compare their list with that of another pair who has worked on the same problem or a different one. As a group, they should challenge themselves to add ideas to the original lists.

4. Students choose a different topic to brainstorm with a partner. How long will it take them to brainstorm 25 ideas? 50 ideas?

5. Students come up with a new topic for others to brainstorm. They should survey the class to see how many different solutions to the problem the group can come up with. In this activity, the whole group is involved in brainstorming at the same time. When students meet each other, they propose solutions to each other's problems and receive ideas in return.

A Structure for Brainstorming: Teaching Tip

The following outline offers a scheme for moving from independent to collaborative work, particularly for brainstorming activities.

1. Students work independently to record answers.

2. Student work in pairs to compare answers. Which items can they borrow from each other?

3. Partners meet with another pair. Students compare answers. What new items can they offer each other?

4, Students work in groups of six or eight. Which item can each student borrow from anyone else in the group? What new items can the group brainstorm to add to the list?

5. Students share as a whole class. Which is the most popular answer? Which is unique?

Brainstorming A B C s

Assure students that if they can't think spontaneously of a word or a phrase for a particular letter (e.g., X, Y, and Z are often more troublesome), they can do research using a dictionary or the Internet or "borrow" answers from others.

Brainstorming items in alphabetical order can lead students to practise and use divergent thinking skills. The alphabetical framework helps students to access prior knowledge about a theme or a topic, but also encourages them to think of words or phrases that might not be immediately obvious. Brainstorming alphabetical lists can be a meaningful collaborative activity as two or more students bounce ideas off each other.

- **C Is for Caring**

Invite students to review the "Caring Classroom A B C" line master (page 151). For ease of reference, the alphabet is summarized here. Students can discuss how they think these words connect to caring classroom communities. What other alphabetical words might they add to this list?

A	Acceptance	B	Belonging	C	Caring
D	Dynamic	E	Equality	F	Fun
G	Groups	H	Harmony	I	Inquiry
J	Justice	K	Kindness	L	Listening
M	Meetings	N	Negotiation	O	Order
P	Perseverance	Q	Questions	R	Respect
S	Safety	T	Trust	U	Understanding
V	Voice	W	Welcome	X	eXtra special
Y	Yes!	Z	Zero tolerance for bullying		

- **Basic Brainstorming**

Students can work with one or two classmates to brainstorm an alphabetical list on a topic of their choice. Some topics to consider include things we read, things we use numbers for, foods, animals, place names, book titles, authors, and book characters. An alphabet grid appears as a line master in the Appendixes.

- **Cooperative Alphabet Books**

Once students have brainstormed an alphabetical list on any topic, they can work collaboratively to assemble a cooperative book, where each student contributes a page. Younger children might be limited to labelling the page with one or two words (e.g., Andy, Brendan, Callum, Dimitri). Older children can use a syntactic pattern that is repeated throughout, for example, "Alysse read an amazing adventure book with her aunt in Australia." The alphabet book is also a useful format for presenting information about a topic. For example, an alphabet book about Canadian geography might include information about the Atlantic Ocean, British Columbia, the Canadian Shield, and Dartmouth.

Choral Dramatization

When we read a poem on a page, it is nothing more than black ink on white paper. By reading the poem aloud, we can make it come to life through the voice. By experimenting with different ways of reading the poem aloud, students can give further meaning to the poem. As they work with others to assign different parts to different group members, to explore how to say the lines, and to rehearse ways to present the poem, they can animate a poem and give meaning through choral dramatization.

Students can work in a group of four or five to read one of the rhymes about the moon (see the "Moon Rhymes" line master next page) or another nursery rhyme chosen by the group. The goal is to read the rhyme aloud 10 different ways. One person can be the leader to help organize the group.

Ten Ways to Read a Poem Together

1. *Echo reading.* The leader reads one line; the group echoes what the leader says.
2. *Alternate reading.* The leader reads one line, the group reads the second line, and so on. The group is divided in half, each reading the lines alternately. The group is divided in half again (e.g., boys/girls, January–June birthdays/July–December birthdays, by even and odd birth dates).
3. *Cloze technique.* The leader reads each line, omitting the final word. The group joins in to say the word. The activity is repeated, with the leader omitting additional words.
4. *Unison.* The group reads the poem aloud together at the same time.
5. *Pitch.* The poem is read in unison, the group starting with a whisper and gradually getting louder and louder. The poem is read in unison, the group starting in a loud voice and gradually getting softer and softer.
6. *Pace.* The poem is read in unison, the group first reading the poem slowly and gradually increasing speed. The poem is read in unison, the group first reading the poem quickly and gradually decreasing speed.
7. *Hand clapping.* The poem is read at a rhythmic pace, accompanied by a clapping rhythm. Students work with a partner to play Pat-a-Cake as they say the poem together.
8. *As a round.* The group divides into two. One group begins to say the poem in unison. The second group begins to say the poem in unison after the first group has finished the first line. Both groups will finish at a different time. The "round" activity is repeated with three or four groups, or individuals starting at a different time.
9. *Assigning a line.* Each person in the group is assigned a line or part of a line (or a word). The group rehearses the poem, with each person contributing his or her part.
10. *Only a word.* The group sits in a circle. The poem is read with each person reading one word in turn.

As a group, students decide the best way to read the poem together to present to others. As they rehearse the choral dramatization, members need to consider how each will stand, what gestures, movement, and sound effects to add, and how to achieve an effective ending. It might be interesting for students to compare their presentation with that of a group that has worked on the same rhyme.

Moon Rhymes

How many different ways can you read one of these rhymes aloud?

Rhyme 1
Sippity sup, sippity sup,
Bread and milk from a china cup,
Bread and milk from a bright silver spoon,
Made of a piece of the bright silver moon!
Sippity sup, sippity sup,
Sippity, sippity sup!

Rhyme 2
There was an old woman tossed up in a basket
Nineteen times as high as the moon;
Where she was going, I couldn't but ask it,
For in her hand she carried a broom.

"Old Woman, Old Woman, Old Woman," said I
"O wither, O wither, O wither, so high?"
"To brush the cobwebs off the sky!
And I'll be back again by and by."

Rhyme 3
The moon has a face like a clock in the hall;
    She shines on thieves on the garden wall,
On streets and fields and harbor quays,
    And birds asleep in the forks of the trees.

The squalling cat and the squeaking mouse,
    The howling dog by the door in the house,
The bat that lies in bed at noon,
    All love to be out by the light of the moon.

Rhyme 4
Girls and boys,
    come out to play
The moon doth shine,
    As bright as day.
Leave your supper,
    And leave your sleep,
Come play with your friends
    Along the street.

Rhyme 5
Listen to the tree bear
Crying in the night
Crying for his mother
In the pale moonlight.
What will his mother do
When she hears the baby cry?
She'll tuck him in his cocoa-pod
And sing a lullaby.

Rhyme 6
Hey diddle, diddle,
    The cat and the fiddle
The cow jumped over the moon;
    The little dog laughed
To see such sport,
    And the dish ran away with the spoon.

Rhyme 7
The moon shines high,
The moon shines low,
Painting the world
With a silvery glow.

Moon travels through
The nighttime sky
Painting the world
With a moonbeam eye.

Rhyme 8
The Man in the Moon as he sails in the sky
Is a very remarkable skipper,
But he made a mistake when he tried to take
A drink of milk from the Dipper.

He dipped right out of the Milky Way
And slowly and carefully filled it;
The Big Bear growled and the Little Bear howled
And frightened him so that he spilled it.

Pembroke Publishers © 2011 *Creating Caring Classrooms* by Kathleen Gould Lundy and Larry Swartz   ISBN 978-1-55138-270-8

Further Explorations with Choral Dramatization

Here are some alternative ways to experience choral dramatization techniques:

- The class can choose poems on a particular theme or topic, for example, funny poems, animal poems, nature poems, Halloween poems, or poems about peace. Each group of four or five can choose one poem to explore before presenting it to others.
- As in the activity above, you can choose a poem by a particular poet or from a particular poetry anthology.
- The class works with a longer poem. Each verse or section of the poem can be assigned to a different group. Once groups have rehearsed and revised their choral dramatization, each can present their work together.
- Each group is given the same poem. Members of the group decide how to present the piece using choral dramatization techniques. Once rehearsed, groups can compare how they completed the task and work towards a presentation.
- Once prepared, the class can present their choral dramatizations to another class or in an assembly. Decisions will have to be made about how to order the presentations, arrange group members on stage or in the large space, and how to address the audience appropriately.

The line master "Assessing Your Work with Choral Dramatization" (next page) provides students with a tool for self-assessment.

Literature Circles

In our lives, we often like to tell others about what we have read. In our enthusiasm to share books, we can retell the story or parts of the story, talk about the characters, tell what we think about the book and how it was written, and reveal what went on in our heads when we read the book. When we talk to others about our reading experiences, we can share our own understanding and perceptions of a book, clarify ideas we found confusing, develop new understandings based on the perceptions offered by others in the group, and take part in a shared experience.

Usually for literature circles, students gather with other members of the class who have read the same book, such as a novel. The students can discuss any aspect of their reading—perceptions, questions, responses, predictions, and opinions—in order to participate in an enjoyable experience that can extend their reading lives.

Literature circles allow students to critically question the texts they are reading and listen for responses that might be different from their own. The activity allows students to "talk themselves into understanding." They come to a deeper comprehension because they are asking questions that they really want the answers to. The teacher is not setting the agenda for learning—the students are—and, in this way, they are taking charge of what they need and want to know.

Here are some guidelines for student participation in a literature circle.

- Each group member has a copy of the book to be discussed.
- Along with the teacher, students determine how much text will need to be read each day to prepare for the meeting.

Assessing Your Work with Choral Dramatization

The following outline can be used to assess your work with choral dramatization.

	Not Yet	Sometimes	Always
1. I contributed ideas and offered suggestions to prepare the choral dramatization.	☐	☐	☐
2. I supported the contributions of other members of the group.	☐	☐	☐
3. I experimented with pitch, pause, and pace to make the reading more effective.	☐	☐	☐
4. I was familiar and confident with my part in the ensemble.	☐	☐	☐
5. I worked well to revise and rehearse the presentation.	☐	☐	☐
6. I was aware of the audience, focusing my delivery to reach the audience.	☐	☐	☐
7. I experimented with gestures and movements to improve the presentation.	☐	☐	☐
8. I enjoyed working on the activity.	☐	☐	☐

Pembroke Publishers © 2011 *Creating Caring Classrooms* by Kathleen Gould Lundy and Larry Swartz ISBN 978-1-55138-255-5

- Students record their thoughts about the reading in a journal. They can summarize, raise questions, prepare drawings, reflect on personal experiences that were inspired by the reading, offer opinions about what they read, and transcribe interesting words or passages from the story.
- Students need to be prepared to meet with fellow group members by reading the assigned text, writing in their journal, and fulfilling their assigned role in the discussion. They can assume different roles each time they meet for discussion.

The *facilitator* helps the group to stay on task, helps keeps the conversation going, gives points for others to add to, and encourages everyone to speak.

The *questioner* presents puzzling issues.

The *reteller* summarizes the day's reading for the group.

The *instigator* raises issues for the group to discuss based on the day's reading.

The *linguist* draws attention to interesting words or passages in the book, making note of page numbers.

The *literary artist* chooses an event or mood conveyed in the reading and illustrates it for the group.

Be sure to emphasize that as a group member discussing a book, a student is expected to

- refer to notes made in a journal
- refer to the book, when appropriate
- express how and why she or he feels a certain way
- add to individual speakers' comments with respect
- ask questions for clarification and for wondering
- pay attention when someone speaks, without interrupting
- allow for differences of opinion

These sentence stems, which can be shared with students, can help guide literature circle conversations:

"Let's discuss why …"
"Tell us what you mean by …"
"I think you're saying …"
"I'm wondering …"
"Could you explain what you mean by …"
"Let's look in the book …"
"Do you think that …"
"I agree …"
"I disagree …"
"I'm confused about …"
"I'd like to add …"
"Tell us why you think that …"

You can encourage students to engage in self-assessment by providing them with copies of the "Assessing Your Work in Literature Circles" line master (next page). Especially the first three statements point to the importance of collaboration in literature circles.

Assessing Your Work in Literature Circles

	Not Yet	Sometimes	Always
1. I come prepared for literature circle discussions.	☐	☐	☐
2. I listen when other members of the group speak.	☐	☐	☐
3. I make equal contributions to the group discussion.	☐	☐	☐
4. I offer opinions about the book.	☐	☐	☐
5. I change my opinion about the book based on the discussion.	☐	☐	☐
6. I am able to retell parts of the story.	☐	☐	☐
7. I comment on the author's style and use of language.	☐	☐	☐
8. I refer to specific parts of the text (or read aloud to verify a point).	☐	☐	☐
9. I relate the book to my own experiences.	☐	☐	☐
10. I enjoy working in literature circles.	☐	☐	☐

My strengths in the literature circle include

_____

_____

Areas I still need to work on include

_____

_____

I benefit from participating in literature circles because

_____

_____

Pembroke Publishers © 2011 *Creating Caring Classrooms* by Kathleen Gould Lundy and Larry Swartz   ISBN 978-1-55138-270-8

Collaborative Writing: Ten Experiences

Students who have participated in literature circles can now work together on creative and collaborative writing projects that have a specific purpose and are connected to what students are learning in the classroom. Just like there needs to be differing roles in literature circles, collaborative writing requires students to share the work as well. In *Co-Authoring in the Classroom: Creating an Environment for Effective Collaboration*, Helen Dale writes, "Writing together allows students to work through the writing process in a social context in which they can both see the variations possible in areas like brainstorming and organizing and also experience the recursiveness of the writing process" (p. 70).

Collaboration offers support for writers of varying strengths as students share their own particular ways of writing and composing. Working together on specific writing events allows students to pool their ideas and feed off each other's strengths and interests.

1. Create an advertising campaign for a school event.

Students, as a group, decide on an event to be advertised and decide upon the medium in which to share the materials (e.g., a CD, a video, an oral presentation, posters).

2. Design a school handbook.

Groups of six to eight decide on an issue that has relevance to the school, perhaps bullying or the environment. Group members research the issue using community and school libraries as well as the Internet to gather resources. The group writes a handbook and works alongside school administrators to publish and distribute it throughout the school community.

3. Publish a school newspaper.

A group can work together to publish a class or school newspaper. Members begin by deciding on the newspaper's length and the sections that need to be included. They are assigned or volunteer for roles of writers, editors, designers, proofreaders, and so on. Students work alone or with others to prepare their pieces to be compiled in the newspaper. Depending on length, copies can be distributed to others in the school or posted online.

4. Write a script for a short play.

Students can choose a theme and work with others to write, rehearse, and present a short script. Ideas for the script can come from significant issues in the classroom or school. Scenarios from novels or other genres of children's literature are also suitable sources for writing scripts. Collaboration can happen at each stage of working towards a performance of the script. Students should be encouraged to take on different roles, including acting, directing, and creating a set and props.

5. Prepare for an informative debate.

Two groups select a topic they would like to debate. (For example: Cell phones should be banned in public places; there should be a rigorous dress code in schools.) Each group picks a side (for or against). The groups need time to gather information about the topic, brainstorm their arguments, and gather evidence to support their point of view. The debate can be held for an audience, with a moderator or judge helping to organize the proceedings.

6. Conduct a consumer research report.

Students in a group can investigate how garbage leaves their home and school, and how it leaves the community. They can research local recycling practices and prepare a consumer report, which they present to others.

7. Make public address announcements.

Students can take leadership to present announcements over the public address system. Some items to consider include Joke of the Day, birthday celebrations, fundraising events, extracurricular activities, "This day in history" reports, and current events. A schedule can be organized so that different teams work to prepare the announcements that will be delivered over the public address system. It is important that students prepare a written script and rehearse the oral presentation of the announcements.

8. Write reviews.

Students can write reviews of a book, a movie, a television show, an advertisement to be shared with others. An alternative way to do this is to have students interview others to get their opinions about an item. Findings can be displayed online, in posters, or in a collaborative book.

9. Create attention-grabbing bulletin-board displays.

Groups of students can work together to prepare a bulletin board in the classroom or in the school that helps others pay attention to an issue or topic or perhaps celebrates a theme or curriculum topic that has been studied in the classroom. Students should consider: "How can we balance the visuals as well as items with written texts? What is the best way to focus an audience's attention on the information and message on the display?"

10. Prepare a class publication.

The class can prepare a publication that includes entries from every student. This publication can be a celebration of a theme or topic that has been investigated in class and have a variety of genres included. Alternatively, students can create an anthology of poetry, fables, opinions, and personal narratives. Copies of the anthology can be shared with parents, other classes, or school library users.

Creating a pattern book is another option. Each member contributes by complying with a pattern, as in a picture book such as *The Important Book* by Margaret Wise Brown or *Brown Bear, Brown Bear, What Do You See?* by Bill

Martin Jr. and Eric Carle. Consider the alphabet pattern for this collaborative publishing project (e.g., an alphabet of places, of book titles, of authors' names). (See Brainstorming A B C s, page 81.)

Collaborative Writing Events: Tips

Recommend that student writing groups adopt the following practices:

- In addition to a group writing folder, each member has a personal writing folder that includes resources, draft writing samples, and final published pieces.
- Members keep a log that tracks the group's progress over time as they work collaboratively to prepare and present their work.
- Members spend time brainstorming and recording ideas using a graphic organizer such as a web or a chart.
- Members consider a balance of responsibility: How can each member contribute to the collaborative activity in an equitable way?
- Members keep in mind that collaborative writing events involve negotiation, problem-solving, and listening. At all times group members consider how to contribute ideas, to receive the ideas of others, to seek clarification from others, to challenge others, and to be respectful of ideas with which they might not agree.
- Members keep self-assessment checklists or journals to help consider their involvement in the project and how well they worked with others.

Student Self-Assessment: Working in Groups

How successful were you when working with others to discuss a topic or complete an activity? Complete the following statements to consider your involvement in groups.

	Always	Sometimes	Not Yet
1. I worked well to complete the activity	☐	☐	☐
2. I contributed ideas to the group	☐	☐	☐
3. I respected and received the ideas of others	☐	☐	☐
4. I was frustrated working in the group	☐	☐	☐

5. A role I enjoy taking when working in groups:

☐ Leader   ☐ Contributor   ☐ Peacemaker   ☐ Enabler   ☐ Organizer

6. My group worked well together because _____

_____

_____

7. I enjoy working in groups because _____

_____

_____

8. I am not fond of working in groups because _____

_____

_____

9. Something I could do better when working in groups is _____

_____

_____

10. Something I would like to say about working in groups is _____

_____

_____

Pembroke Publishers © 2011 *Creating Caring Classrooms* by Kathleen Gould Lundy and Larry Swartz   ISBN 978-1-55138-270-8

The Shine Project: Communication, Collaboration, and Compassion Meet in an Arts-Based Project

by Raymond Peart

Raymond is a multi-generational Canadian, born and raised in Toronto. Working with the burdens and joys of being a Black male, as well as possessing a victim's narrative of being bullied, Raymond seeks to evoke in his work the ethic of sharing knowledge, developing leaders, and promoting critical thought through compassion. He holds an undergraduate degree in Fine Arts and English, and a masters degree in Education. He is currently working on his Ph.D. in the Faculty of Education at York University.

In 2010, something wonderful happened. In collaboration with Shoreham Public School, the students of York University's Urban Diversity Consecutive Teaching Program and the administrators of Shoreham Public School came together to create a free, after-school arts program that took place in the Shoreham Public School gymnasium. Under the guidance and leadership of Kathy Gould Lundy, the program offered a series of process drama workshops that focused on the theme "Who am I?"

Students in Grades 4/5 joined teacher candidates to collaborate in a drama-based project in which everyone had an opportunity to learn from and about each other. For four after-school sessions, the students explored themes and ideas found in a picture book, *The Name Jar*. Together, they played games, created tableaux in response to the book, spoke and wrote in role, shared personal stories, and gained an empathetic understanding of the main character's personal dilemma. All the students—both young and older—learned about drama. They became involved in a story from the inside perspective. Administrators, course directors, and board of education personnel took part in all the sessions. The York University students gained valuable insights in how to teach drama by doing the work and then debriefing what happened after the end of each afternoon workshop.

Three key themes blossomed from The Shine Project:

1. Collaboration is compulsory to success.
2. Democracy must be made visible within the relational experiences of students.
3. Leadership cannot flourish without compassion.

Inclusive and Sustaining Paradigm

"This partnership created an opportunity for our boys and girls in Grades 4 and 5 to open up and let their imaginations flow through movement and verbal and non-verbal expression. Being in role of other complex heroes in stories allowed them to juxtapose their own private voices with an imaginary 'ginormous' world and yet remain safe and intact with this world. Vice-Principal Harpreet Ghuman and I initially recruited students to participate in this program. We assured the students that we were going to participate with them. This factor added a dimension of comfort, trust, and excitement. They were thrilled to participate, commit to a story, and learn about themselves and others through drama."
—Shosh Brenner, principal, Shoreham P.S.

Imagine a world in which people listen to each other and learn from one another. Imagine a space in which teachers, mothers, school trustees, fathers, daughters, high-ranking officials from boards and ministries, sons, aunts, uncles, prospective teachers, graduate students, and professors stand together eager to learn from and listen to one another. In such a location, space is unrefined, uncomfortable, and unpredictable. The texture of space and time worked together to create a moment of perfect imperfection, a space in which experiences, actions, and responses were supported by and for the collective.

Inclusiveness necessitated dialogue. We learned to listen to all voices and all ideas. Ensuring everyone's contribution to the meaning-making process was paramount to the architecture of the program.

The starting point for our partnership was to ask, "What do you need and how can we work with you to get there?" Shosh Brenner, the principal of the school, and Harpreet Ghuman, the vice-principal, said they wanted their students to be enriched through the arts. Jacquie Spence, the York University course director, said that her teacher candidates needed to have a hands-on experience to find out about how to set up a drama program so that they could see learning through drama in action.

The questions were answered, so we went ahead and made it happen. The project was driven entirely by the teacher candidates who insisted on everyone being present and participating fully from the first session to the last, and who acted as side coaches to ensure that all got involved.

The Democracy of Voice

The Shine Project became something unexpected. It taught us that the sharing of one's identity or culture can never be about passing an institutional view of what those identities should look like; rather, the process of sharing should encourage moments of democratic opportunity in which each participant—student and teacher—is willing to address the gaps in the audience—to make the other "literate." I define *literacy* in its most expanded sense: knowledge that allows the subject to create a meaningful experience. The process of making each other literate is to bring the subject into a dialogue; both the speaker and the recipient of that speech enter into a joint venture. Such a task requires the reconstruction of relationships between administrators, teachers, students, and other members of the community. Towards this end, literacy became a prominent vehicle through which the students and teacher candidates learned from one another. Such a platform renegotiated how voices created meaning by recognizing and putting into practice acts of cohesion that overtly—but not mockingly—redefined roles.

On the very first day, the elementary students seemed to have a solid understanding of what drama was. One student said, "It provides people with an opportunity to be someone else, but all the time they know that they are 'playing' at being another person." The elementary students also seemed clear about why drama should be part of education: "It allows us to see different perspectives." "It is about learning about people's feelings and thoughts." The student teachers were impressed by the capacity of the younger students to articulate the learning that could occur in and through drama.

The elementary students became the teachers in significant and surprising ways. The Shine Project taught us that good teachers need not fear locating themselves in the learning processes of their students; good teachers bridge subject, self, student, and environment in ways that are necessary and that illuminate the facility for which learning can take place without borders.

Leadership Cannot Exist Without Compassion

There is no place where time stands still. Clocks do not stop, the sun never ceases to rise, and birds do not hang motionless in the air. Laughter never hangs suspended in the air. Yet we often approach children as if they have all the time in the world, and such an attitude mutes the urgency of many of their contexts—contexts that may be strewn by inequity, silence, and bullying. The commitment of the program emerged from an urgency among the creators and facilitators to address gaps that we felt would ultimately serve the students in their life journey. Part of the task in fulfilling goals of anti-oppression, anti-discrimination, and ultimately, social justice is coming to the awareness that we are all trying to get through this world in the best way that we know. Bringing ourselves to re-imagine and empathize with the challenges that administrators face daily begins to commit us to a path of compassion in which administrators are not seen as antagonists, but as people who have a difficult job to perform.

The administrators of the school, as well as the course directors and board personnel, did not just drop in to the sessions to observe—they participated fully in every drama session. They interacted with the children and challenged themselves to become involved in the story and to listen to the student voices that were shaping it into something marvellous. Their role was key to our success. The Shine Project succeeded because those who participated in it believed in it with their cores. The principal and vice-principal not only shared their experiences and knowledge with the planners, but became active participants with the students. Within that simple act, their leadership showed us that commitment must take place at all levels—and that we can never think ourselves too busy to smile, learn, struggle, and succeed with our students.

One teacher candidate spoke of his fear of doing this kind of work in the classroom. "What the students taught me," he said, "was that they want to take risks—they want to learn this way. Why should I, because I am afraid, deny them this experience?"

"The SHINE program in its very essence to me represents emancipatory pedagogy. For our students, it celebrated their identity, history, power, and the limitless potential of imagination. It allowed us to hear the voices and stories that are often ignored or are silenced. For those leading the program, there was, at the centre, a platform, a validation, and above all, a profound belief in each and every child's potential. The end result was an inspirational and enriching teaching and learning experience for all involved. We will never forget the insights gained and the friendships made; the experiences about how to be more human we will take with us into the future."
—Harpreet Ghuman, vice-principal, Shoreham P.S.

And so there sits in a small room, a group of 16 people—a marriage of teacher candidates, a graduate student, board administrators, and university educators—who are planning and begin to ponder how this program will turn out. The more seasoned educators and administrators talk about the need for snacks. But there is no money. The teacher candidates talk of a bake sale and a casino night to raise funds for these students. We talk of an awards ceremony. But there are no funds. We talk about putting in our own money without want of reimbursement. We talk, perhaps teetering towards a heated discussion, but this is necessary because it lights the fire from which all of us will shine. Time begins to run out. But there is a plan … and hope.

We have unbound ourselves from the legacy of traditional leadership. We all have ownership, yet we are all students. In this space, there are no teachers; we are all the same. Human.

On the final evening of celebration, a child to whom I have never spoken hugs me and then runs off. I am content on this evening because she has told me, through no words, that we did a good thing—that we did a good thing. We eat, we laugh, and we talk as companions who have little in common, save for our common goal as students who have helped to inspire new education. We SHINE.

Chapter 4

Building Compassion

My friends, love is better than anger. Hope is better than fear. Optimism is better than despair. So let us be loving, hopeful and optimistic. And we will change the world.

—Final public message from Jack Layton, leader of the Official Opposition in Canadian Parliament, who died August 22, 2011

If you visit the United States Holocaust Memorial Museum in Washington, D.C., you can go to the gift store and purchase a T-shirt, a carry-all bag, or a rubber wrist bracelet with this slogan: **"What You Do Matters."** But having the words on a wrist bracelet is one thing; putting these words into action is quite another. And it's one thing to put these words into action, but quite another to help students understand that what they do, what they say, and what they believe, matters.

Telling Stories to Build Compassion

"It is beneficial for members of a society to see themselves as bound to one another by similar weaknesses and needs as well as by similar capacities for achievement."

—From *Cultivating Humanity: A Classical Defence of Reform in Liberal Education* by Martha C. Nussbaum (Cambridge, MA: Harvard University Press, 1997, p. 92)

As Martha C. Nussbaum writes in *Cultivating Humanity*, one thing that is important in the establishment of caring classrooms is for students to achieve "an accurate awareness of our common vulnerability" (p. 91). This knowledge and sensitivity can be achieved by giving students opportunities to tell their stories—not just of their successes but also of their failures. Telling personal stories often increases compassion in classrooms as students begin to see that suffering and loss bind people to one another and make us more aware of the human condition in all of its complexity.

Personal storytelling can grow out of literature circles, drama sessions, or media events. Delving into the challenges and motivations of characters in novels, films, short stories, and plays can also be a way for teachers to build the compassionate classroom. As students talk about the characters whom they meet, watch, or embody, they find ways of identifying with their situations and begin to connect their personal stories to those fictional lives.

The academic, artistic, and social work of the classroom is dependent on many things: what the student brings to the classroom in terms of background knowledge, experience, attitude, and learning style and what the teacher models, expects, wants to happen, knows, values, and provides in terms of resources. So much of the work is dependent on the willingness of teachers to listen to their students, to reflect back to them their identities in the books and resources that they choose, and to find ways to celebrate the diversity before them in terms of learning style, language, race, sexual orientation, gender, and cultural and class background.

To acknowledge, learn about, and celebrate diversity is a necessary part of curricular learning in the classroom. As difficult and challenging as it is, the work needs to be done if we want to empower students to understand the issues that have affected people in the past and help them find their voices today to change their lives and the world around them in the future. It is important, therefore, to make our classrooms places where students experience equity as part of their daily lives—where they can be part of a community that affirms diversity and promotes equity. It is crucial for all of us to create classrooms that reflect our students' interests, racial and cultural backgrounds, family relationships, special needs and abilities.

How can we teach compassion to young people? How can we help students be accountable for their actions? How can we stretch and challenge those with an I-don't-care attitude to become more caring human beings? In the book *Don't Laugh at Me*, Steve Seskin and Allen Shamblin tell readers: "You don't have to be my friend, but is [this] too much to ask? Don't laugh at me. Don't call me names. Don't get your pleasure from my pain." Conflicts and differences of opinion are part of life, and challenging students to deal with conflicts and differences is important work if we want them to move beyond name calling and abusive behavior. Changing behaviors is hard to do, but from 9 a.m. to 3 p.m. we can work hard to help students grow, step by step, to be respectful and accepting of one another.

We cannot just snap our fingers and tell the students to "be compassionate." Building compassion means that we are working with the stuff of emotions and beliefs, as well as assumptions that have become part of the way in which students see the world. To change the way that we all see one another and ourselves requires mutual trust—students trusting the teacher and trusting one another.

So much determines the attitudes and beliefs that become part of young people's living. Home life, community, identities, culture, environment, and media that weave through their developmental stages of growth influence who the students are becoming (and might become). The opportunities that young people have had working with others to experience the sharing of thoughts and feelings, the solving of problems, and the negotiation of ideas can move students into developing empathetic, compassionate behaviors. Providing students with opportunities to discuss books and world events helps. Providing opportunities for students to reveal and expose personal stories helps. Allowing students to respond and react to the stories and ideas of others helps. Asking students to actively engage with difficult material to find new understandings also helps.

The Dalai Lama has proclaimed, "It is not enough to be compassionate, you must act." In our classrooms, we can find ways for students to act compassionately. When students communicate, collaborate, and create together, they are in an active mode that helps them act compassionately. In this way, we are closer and closer to creating caring classrooms that matter. Moreover, we are moving the students forward to being compassionate human beings during their life's journeys.

"I was very fortunate in having lived as a child and as a young boy in an environment where there were many people I could revere, people concerned with problems of inner life, of spirituality and integrity. People who have shown great compassion and understanding of other people."

—Abraham Heschel

Acting to Make a Difference

One Wingbeat at a Time

Noble Peace Prize laureate Wangari Maathai shared this inspirational story when she addressed 7000 educators from around the world in Montreal at an annual Botanic Gardens Conservation International conference. Maathai founded the Green Belt Movement, an organization that provides income, education, and sustenance to millions of people in Kenya through the planting of trees. She has been honored with numerous awards for her work as an environmental activist and as an advocate for civil society and women's rights.

A Canadian picture book version of the story of the hummingbird has been created by Michael Nicoll Yahgulanaas, a Haida artist. The Tsimshian people of the North Pacific recognize the hummingbird to be a joyful messenger, delivering hope and healing during time of sorrow and pain.

See anime "Flight of the Hummingbird" by Michael Nicoll Yahgulanaas on YouTube.

The story of a small hummingbird determined to put out a forest fire is told by the Quechua people of Ecuador and Peru. While other animals stand by, bemoaning their inability to stop the fire, the hummingbird actively strives to fight it. Hummingbird demonstrates that it is not always the largest or the loudest that can do the most good. Her efforts remind us that the one who is not afraid to act can make the biggest difference or at least, that trying to do something is worthwhile.

Whatever "message" the students take from the story, they will, it is hoped, understand that the animals of the forest each gave selfish reasons for not helping to put out the forest fire. Can we be compassionate of those who choose not to get involved in a mission? Can we convince those who are reluctant to help out to be compassionate to the cause that others deem to be important?

We hope and expect that students will respond differently to whether Hummingbird was successful in her brave effort to put out the fire. By listening to the viewpoints of others, students will be able to further consider how someone can best take action in times of trouble and how we "do our best" to put forth a compassionate effort even when others do not act in the same way. Considering their own values and the beliefs of others can help move students in their understanding of compassionate behavior.

One version of the story of the hummingbird appears as a line master on the next page. The story will be used as the focus for a number of activities related to putting compassion into action.

1. Respond through writing and talk.

In this activity, adapted from Lynda Hoyt, students use a graphic organizer to write a response after reading a story or listening to a picture book being read out loud. By sharing their response with two classmates, students can discover whether their opinions were similar to or different from their own. This activity works best if students do it in groups of three.

- Students take a blank piece of paper and fold it twice, to make four rectangles. They number the spaces 1, 2, 3, and 4.
- In space 1, students write a short response to the story to consider what it reminded them of, give an opinion, or raise question puzzles.

The Story of the Hummingbird

One day, a terrible fire broke out in a forest. As flames engulfed the huge woodlands, all the animals rushed out of the forest to safety. The snake slithered steadily away. The rabbit hopped, the wolf leapt, and the big bear lumbered out of the forest. Even the birds flew away in a panic.

Frightened by the raging flames and the clouds of dark smoke, the animals ran and ran until they reached the edge of a nearby stream, where they huddled together.

"I can't do anything to put out the fire," hissed the snake.

"What can I do?" asked the rabbit. "The fire is so hot and I am so little."

"The fire is so big," cried the wolf. "I am so frightened."

"My fur will burn!" cried the big bear.

Full of despair, the animals looked back in silence to watch the blazing fire destroying their homes. How sad and frightened and powerless they felt! Each thought that there was nothing they could do to destroy the monstrous fire.

Except for one tiny hummingbird.

Hummingbird decided she would do something to help. She flew as fast as she could and swooped into the stream. She picked up a single drop of water and returned to the forest and put it on the fire. She then went back to the stream and gathered a drop of water again and again. Hummingbird kept going back and forth, back and forth. All the animals watched in disbelief as the brave bird continued her work drop by drop by drop.

"Why are you bothering?" said the snake.

"Your wings will burn," said the rabbit.

"It's too much. You are too little," said the wolf.

The animals just stood around, but Hummingbird carried on, gathering drops of water one by one. The bird noticed how hopeless they all looked.

The big bear growled, "Hummingbird, you are so little. What do you think you are doing?"

Hummingbird did not stop to argue. Without losing a beat, she looked back and said, "I am doing everything I can."

Pembroke Publishers © 2011 *Creating Caring Classrooms* by Kathleen Gould Lundy and Larry Swartz ISBN 978-1-55138-270-8

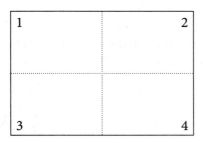

- Students exchange papers with another person in the group. Students read the response in space 1 and then write a response to it in space 2. What did the response in space 1 encourage them to think about? Ask students to consider whether they agree or disagree with what was written.
- The activity is repeated. Students read both responses on the sheet they receive and write a response in space 3.
- The sheet is returned to the person who wrote the first response. Students read all three responses on the sheet and write a new response in space 4.
- In groups students discuss the story, using their written responses to frame the discussion.

With thanks to Ernest Agbuya's Grade 6 class

> ① When I heard about the humming bird, I thought that even though the humming bird wanted to help, did he realize that even if he carried a lot of water at different times the fire spread.
>
> ② I think it's great that the Hummingbird tried to save the forest.
>
> ③ The humming bird was very determined to make a difference, and was going to do every thing he could. Go, bird go!
>
> ④ The hummingbird was great and thoughtful for trying to make a difference even though he might not do anything that helpful but he at least attempted to do so.

How a group of three students responded to the hummingbird story

2. Discuss as a whole class.

As a class students discuss the story. The following key questions can be used to guide the discussion.

- What lesson do you think can be learned from this story?
- Do you think Hummingbird's attempts to put out the fire were foolish?
- What puzzles or questions come to mind?
- What other stories of bravery does this story remind you of?
- What does the statement "I am doing everything I can" mean to you?
- In what real-life ways can we put Hummingbird's philosophy into action?

3. Create art images.

Students can create an illustration that they think could be used in a picture book version of this story. Students' images can be assembled into a class publication for others to read. One suggestion is to do torn paper art, where students use a variety of colored paper to create their scene—no scissors allowed.

"It's Cool to Care!"

Me to We, founded in 2008 by brothers Marc and Craig Kielburger, sponsors camps and overseas voyages for volunteer youth who want to make positive change in the world. When participating in any of the *Me to We* events, young people learn how to have a social and environmental impact, thus building a capacity to be compassionate world citizens. Information can be found at www. metowe.com.

4. Retell the story.

Students work in pairs or small groups to retell the story, with each person contributing one sentence as the storytelling unfolds. Once the retelling is completed, students can revisit a printed version of the text to determine how successfully they included details from the story. They can add or change information.

Repeat the activity by having the students tell the story from the first person point of view of one of the animals or perhaps the hummingbird.

> 4. I wish to see people living the message of this story instead of going with the flow and not showing the courage to stand on his/her own feet. We can't make a difference unless we are brave.

One group's consolidated response

5. Create tableaux.

Students work in groups of three or four to retell the story of the hummingbird in still images. To begin, invite the students to create one scene from the story; then, tell them to create two scenes, one before and one after. Students can also retell the story using five images. Each picture can be given a title.

6. Dramatize the story.

Students can work in groups to dramatize the story in one of the following ways:

- story theatre techniques (e.g., narrator(s) and actors)
- tableaux and narration
- mime and movement only (perhaps with musical accompaniment)
- improvisation of the story, where all characters have a speaking part
- puppets

Let students choose which method they would like to work with. Alternatively, each group can be assigned a different strategy for presenting the story. Give time to rehearse the play which can be shared with an audience.

Building Compassion Through Script Fragments

With thanks to colleagues Bob Barton and Debbie Nyman, and to Jim Giles, Elementary Teachers' Federation of Ontario

The line master titled "Script Fragments" (page 101) features script fragments selected from *More Than a Play*, a resource available through the Elementary Teachers' Federation of Ontario. This book is a collection of nine short plays that have been written by top Canadian playwrights. The short scripts explore equity and current social justice issues, such as gender bias, ageism, disability, cyberbullying, racism, and homophobia. As students work with others to read any of these scripts aloud and prepare to present and perform them, they come to understand the complexities of eliminating intolerance and prejudice in the world. The plays in this resource offer stories and themes that demonstrate how young people deal with inequities.

As students work with the scripts and bring these scenes to life, they come to empathize with the characters who are dealing with troubling situations. By stepping into the shoes of others and discussing the issues, students can come to understand how these characters might feel; they can develop compassionate understanding of real-life situations that connect to script themes.

For the next activities that involve students in interpreting text, provide students with pages of dialogue lines and invite them to approach the lines like a script.

1. Read the lines out loud.

Students read through the lines silently.

Students choose any line to begin with and read through the lines out loud. Once they reach the bottom of the list, they begin to read from the top of the list. In this way, students will not be reading the lines in unison.

Students choose a new line to begin reading. This time, students walk around the room as they read the lines out loud.

Students read the lines in a variety of ways (e.g., changing tempo, mood, or volume).

Students select a line they find intriguing and memorize it.

Script Fragments

1. Sadly, you won't be able to go.

2. Have a little respect for her feelings.

3. Can I trust you?

4. The most important thing is school. Don't you forget!

5. Watch where you're walking.

6. What are you doing here?

7. He promised he'd come.

8. What did you get the medal for?

9. You're looking, but you're not seeing.

10. You're not coming with us?

11. Next time, she better watch out.

12. Is there something wrong?

13. I don't feel right about it.

14. Oh, come on! Am I the only guy who thinks that's weird?

15. How come I didn't know that?

16. Maybe I should say something?

17. Just give me a break.

18. I can't believe it.

19. That's so sad.

20. I hope you're kidding me.

21. It certainly doesn't seem fair but it's still a deal.

22. Look, there's just this feeling I have in the pit of my stomach, I don't even control it, it's just the way I feel, and I'm being honest with you.

23. This has been the longest 15 minutes of my life.

24. You don't know what it's like.

Permission to reprint from *More Than a Play*, published by the Elementary Teachers' Federation of Ontario.

2. Create a scene together.

Students form groups of three and share their lines with others. As a group, they consider an order in which to say their three lines. Students should be encouraged to experiment with different orders until they are satisfied with a scene that works best. Groups work to present a short scene that includes the three lines. They should consider how to give the lines, where the actors will stand or sit, what gestures they will make, and how the scene will begin and end.

3. Share scenes with an audience.

Cue students to perform moments of the scenes they have developed. By being an audience for others, students will have an opportunity to observe the multiple meanings in the words and the variety of interpretations of a single line.

4. Improvise!

Students in pairs are arranged in two rows, A and B, with partners facing each other. Player A is invited to begin by reciting one of the lines. Player B responds to player A by improvising dialogue. The pairs make up a brief scene. The activity is repeated with students in row B delivering the opening lines and students in row A responding, as together they improvise a scene.

Students in row A are directed to move down the line to the left so that each player A faces a new partner. The activity is repeated.

Students continue to encounter new partners by moving down the line. Students are assigned different ways to consider the delivery of their lines: perhaps beginning with a high-five clap, a handshake, a strong emotion, as if said by an angry parent, as if said by the president of a company.

5. Write a scene.

Consider having students work with others to write a short scene that includes one or more script fragments. Once completed, students can rehearse and present their scenes to others.

Social Justice Memories

Invite the students to share a personal experience connected to one of the issues that *More Than a Play* addresses. As noted earlier, issues include racial bias, ableism, ageism, immigration, classism, homophobia, conflict, and cyberbullying. The story that students tell may have happened to them or someone they know. Some students might share stories from books, films and television, and the media that provide examples of one of these issues.

Each playwright featured in *More Than a Play* shares a social justice memory as an introduction to his or her script. These stories can serve as models for students to tell or write their own social justice memories. In the introduction to his short play *The Speech*, playwright David S. Craig shares this social justice memory:

> From grades one to eight, we sat in alphabetical order so I always sat beside a kid named Nicolas Brenton. The class bullies teased Nicolas because he had red hair and loads of freckles. I was scared to say anything to Nicolas because I thought if I did, the

bullies would tease me. So for eight years, I sat behind a kid I never spoke to. I wish I hadn't been so afraid. If I met Nicolas Brenton now, I would apologize.

Invite students to share their stories in small groups. Some may volunteer to share stories with the whole class.

Developing a Personal Philosophy

A Gift of Days: The Greatest Words to Live By, edited by Stephen Alcorn, is a collection of the inspirational words and ideas of noteworthy figures. It celebrates the society of which we're all a part and reminds us that we each have the potential to change the world every day of the year.

The activities listed below provide strategies for students to respond to the quotations featured on the "Quotations About Compassion" line master (next page). Students can share their personal connections to the sayings of others and consider what personal philosophy frames their outlook on life.

1. Respond to the quotations.

Students choose one of the quotations outlined on the list and write a short response that considers these questions:

- What does this quotation mean?
- Why did you choose this quotation?
- What does this quotation invite you to think about?

2. Research other quotations.

A number of quotations are provided on the Internet. Students can choose a topic that interests them and investigate other quotations to share (e.g., quotations about friendship, education, and peace). Which is their favorite?

3. Do further research.

Students can gather research about the source of a quotation. They may find information about why this quotation was created, when it was said, and who the audience was.

4. Prioritize quotations.

Students choose a favorite quotation, perhaps from the list provided. Students then work in groups of five or six with each student contributing a quotation. Students prioritize the items by listing the most significant to the least significant. Groups can then share their choices with other groups.

5. Get into a corner.

Stretched Out on a Line

"Line ups" is an alternative way to offer this activity. Students at one end of the line strongly agree with a statement; students at the other end of the line strongly disagree with a statement.

Call out a statement likely to generate strong opinions. The students consider whether they agree with the statement or not and then arrange themselves into the four corners of the room, each labelled Strongly agree, Agree, Disagree, or Strongly disagree. Groups can discuss the reasons for their choices. The activity is then repeated with a new statement or quotation.

Quotations About Compassion

"Ask not what your country can do for you, but what you can do for your country."
~John F. Kennedy

"Human kindness has never weakened the stamina or softened the fiber of a free people. A nation does not have to be cruel to be tough."
~Franklin D. Roosevelt

"I know for sure that what we dwell on is what we become."
~Oprah Winfrey

"No one can make you feel inferior without your consent."
~Eleanor Roosevelt

"You cannot do a kindness too soon, for you never know how soon it will be too late."
~Ralph Waldo Emerson

"Kind words can be short and easy to speak, but their echoes are truly endless."
~Mother Teresa

"Our attitude toward life determines life's attitude towards us."
~Earl Nightingale

"Our lives begin to end the day we become silent about the things that matter."
~Martin Luther King

"He who lives in harmony with himself lives in harmony with the world."
~Marcus Aurelius

"Better than a thousand hollow words is one word that brings peace."
~Buddha

"To the world you might be one person, but to one person you might be the world."
~J. W. von Goethe

"You cannot teach a person anything. You can only help him discover it within himself."
~Galileo

"Love doesn't make the world go round, love is what makes the ride worthwhile."
~Elizabeth Browning

"Whether you think you can or you think you can't—you are right!"
~Henry Ford

"Well done is better than well said."
~Benjamin Franklin

"Those having torches will pass them on to others."
~Plato

"If you want others to be happy, practice compassion. If you want to be happy, practice compassion."
~Dalai Lama

"There is no one way to be human."
~Robert Fulgham

"Carry out a random act of kindness, with no expectation of reward, safe in the knowledge that one day someone might do the same for you."
~Lady Diana Spencer

"The past, the present and the future are really one: They are today."
~Harriet Beecher Stowe

"In spite of everything I still believe that people are really good at heart."
~Anne Frank

Pembroke Publishers © 2011 *Creating Caring Classrooms* by Kathleen Gould Lundy and Larry Swartz   ISBN 978-1-55138-255-5

6. Present quotations.

Students in pairs are each assigned a quotation to work with. Invite the students to find a way to bring this quotation to life using one or more of the following drama techniques: reading it aloud, creating a still image, using movement. Once students have rehearsed their work, they can present their quotation to others. The presentations can be assembled into a class collective to be shared with a larger audience.

7. Create posters.

Students can choose a quotation and create a poster or banner to visually display it in the classroom or in the school.

8. Make sculptures.

Students are given some modelling clay to create a sculpture that represents one of the quotations. Remind students that their sculptures can be symbolic, rather than literal.

9. Do primary research.

Many people have a personal statement that gives them a philosophy of life. It might be something that a parent or grandparent often repeated, or it might be a quotation that they have read or heard about from the media. As a research project, students can interview one or two adults in the school community or in their family to find out what their favorite motto in life is and why it is important to them. Have students report their findings in a class meeting.

10. Arrive at a mission statement.

Students work in small groups to discuss which quotation they think might serve as a mission statement for their classroom. Groups can offer their choices to the whole group. As a class, the students can choose or compose a philosophical statement for the classroom community.

Spreading the Word: Be Good, Do Good, Encourage Goodness Everywhere

Sample Billboard

Renew someone's faith in mankind.
Smile at them.

Want to hear an uplifting story?
**A guy lets everyone get on the train before him.
The End.**

On Saturday, July 30, 2011, *Toronto Star* reporter Isabel Teotino described an advertising campaign sweeping through Canada's largest cities, encouraging people to be good, do good, and encourage goodness everywhere. The multi-million dollar campaign, dubbed People for Good, aims to promote generosity. Pioneered by two media experts, Mark Sherman and Zulu Alpha Kilo, the project aims to encourage a change in behavior. In the front-page article, the two media executives explain, "the genesis of this was about wanting to do something positive and socially responsible and taking stock of what we do for a living. And what we do for a living is changing attitudes and behaviours."

Sixty media owners donated ad space or air time to promote the mission. The campaign spread throughout the country with messages featured on billboards from Halifax to Vancouver. Besides billboard advertisements, suggestions for good deeds are made on a website (www.peopleforgood.ca) and are made available on a free People for Good iPhone app. Sherman told the reporter: "We can't rely on government to change things, so it's incumbent on each of us as individuals to try and do something. But there is power in the collective of a business, so if we can take our people and capture the power of that collective, important things can be achieved."

So, how does this public initiative translate into the classroom? Here are six classroom "do good" initiatives that students can become involved with.

1. *Discussing the campaign*. Provide students with information about the People for Good initiative. Ask the students questions like these:

- Do you think the intention of the campaign is worthwhile?
- Do you think this money is well spent on such a campaign?
- Can such a campaign make a difference? How?
- How successful might such a campaign be in our community?

2. *Gathering further research*. Students can use the Internet to gather further information about the People for Good campaign. What suggestions are offered online and on the iPhone app for doing good?

3. *Gathering data*. Students can investigate data that validates the success (or not) of this campaign. They can survey others to determine how successful they think such a campaign would be.

4. *Advertisements*. Students can create posters to go up throughout the community. They can use suggestions from the campaign or create new suggestions to spread the word.

5. *Letters to the editor*. Students can write letters to a local newspaper, post information on a blog, or involve other media connections to spread the word of doing good. What arguments and data will they provide to support their views of such a campaign?

6. *"Students for Good" campaign*. In addition to creating posters, students can brainstorm ways to conduct their own "Students for Good" campaign. How might they promote goodness in the classroom, in the school community, outside the school, and beyond the community? How might a blog be useful for this campaign?

It Gets Better Campaign

After a number of tragic suicides by Lesbian Gay Bisexual Transgender students who were bullied in school, syndicated columnist and author Dan Savage and his partner, Terry Miller, uploaded a video to YouTube to inspire hope for LGBT youth facing harassment. The two men spoke openly about the bullying they had suffered as teenagers and how they had both gone on to lead rewarding lives. Their video launched the It Gets Better Project and created a worldwide phenomenon with more than 20 million views in the first three months alone.

The book they edited, *It Gets Better*, is a collection of original essays and testimonials written for teens by celebrities, political leaders, and everyday citizens. Its goal is to indicate to LGBT youth the kind of happiness, potential, and satisfaction their lives can hold if they can but get through the adolescent years.

Advocating Gender Equity

Cheryl Kilodavis wrote the picture book *My Princess Boy* to prompt children and adults to talk about acceptance and unconditional friendship. Kilodavis's son, Dyson, enjoys wearing princess dresses and a tiara crown to school, and as a concerned parent, Kilodavis worried about Dyson being teased and bullied in school settings. Towards the end of the book, she raises some tough questions.

> If you see a Princess Boy …
> Will you laugh at him?
> Will you call him a name?
> Will you play with him?
> Will you like him for who he is?

Seeking answers to these questions can help a community of learners consider their own values and promote acceptance of those considered easy targets for taunting.

Recognizing the unthinkable outcomes of bullying, picture books (see list on page 109) can promote discussions about acceptance and help children—and adults—consider how we can be compassionate with one another. From the book-jacket blurb for *My Princess Boy* readers learn:

> Compassion takes effort. It takes focus. It takes commitment. We need practice. And more practice. And practice again. We are an ecosystem. Our compassion for one another and the broader world is dependent on one another. And when we interconnect, we celebrate the unique person within us all.

See the YouTube interview: My Princess Boy.

Gender equity is a way of thinking. Yes, boys and girls are different from each other. But the differences within any gender are greater than the differences between the two genders. What kind of boy? What kind of girl? For many reasons (e.g., brain differences, nurture and nature, peer and media influence), young children hold strong gender stereotypes for the activities they participate in, the toys they are offered to play with, the clothes they prefer to wear, and the books they choose to read. As educators and parents, we need to support many of the choices the children make, and guide them into being respectful of choices that others make. If we want to help them become caring, compassionate individuals, we must confront them when remarks and attitudes are overtly sexist.

One way to help young people work towards an understanding of social justice, diversity, and equity issues is to have them consider assumptions about boy and girl characteristics and behavior. We can introduce literature that will support and deepen young children's knowledge and assumptions of gender equity and implement activities that will help them consider gender stereotypes. What feelings and thoughts are inspired by the story of William, who wanted a doll to hug and cradle in his arms (*William's Doll*); Princess Smartypants, who did not want to get married because she enjoyed being a Ms. (*Princess Smartypants*); or Dandi Mackall, who was told that she couldn't play in the after-school baseball games because she's a girl (*A Girl Named Dan*)? How might the children react and behave if William, Princess Smartypants, Dandi Mackall, or Dyson Kilodavis were sitting alongside them in the classroom?

When we give students opportunities to share their responses and hear the responses of others, we can support them in critically examining unfair everyday issues pertaining to gender, making informed decisions, empathizing, and engaging in social action.

No matter which strategies are used by teachers, the objective should be to increase awareness and acceptance of the idea that each human being is afforded the right to develop his or her own unique potential. By introducing a curriculum that explores issues of gender stereotyping, we can plant seeds of understanding among children and help them explore practical ways to make a positive impact in the world and be respectful, open-minded, and understanding of individual differences. The curriculum may expose the world of pink and blue bar-coding, but the real task at hand is to bring up active, principled, compassionate people.

1. Blue Jobs, Pink Jobs

Provide students with a sheet folded into four squares. Explain that they are each going to create illustrations for a picture book about occupations. Students create a quick drawing for each of the squares, perhaps a doctor, hairdresser, dancer, and lawyer. Once students have completed their illustrations, survey the class to determine which jobs have been depicted as male, which as female. Students can discuss which genders they think are most commonly associated with each occupation.

2. Advertisements

Display a variety of newspaper or magazine advertisements featuring males and females. Have students discuss whether they think each advertisement supports or breaks a stereotype. What are some positive features of the ad? Does the ad appeal to one gender more than another? How would the advertisement be different if the genders were switched? Is the choice of gender appropriate for the product?

3. Public Service Announcements (PSAs)

Students can view public service announcements created by Concerned Children's Advertisers of Health Canada:

- We are Girls: http://youtu.be/IY_2Lqohj70
- What's Your Thing?: http://youtu.be/OX6qUFm1Hsl

Discuss the purpose of each PSA. Who is the intended audience for each? What do students think the message of this announcement is? How do these PSAs give viewers confidence in their ability to do anything they desire and not be pressured to conform to gender stereotypical roles? Students may be ready to discuss how surroundings might influence how boys and girls think they should behave, look, and feel.

4. Gender T-charts

Divide the students into single-gender groups of three or four. Give each group a sheet of paper and prepare a T-chart. In column 1, students can brainstorm all the things they think they like about being a girl or boy, that is, things that they feel they are good at or admire. In the second column, students can list things they admire about the other gender. Once their T-charts are completed, two groups of mixed gender can meet to compare lists. Encourage students to consider whether the items on the list are true for all, most, or some boys and girls.

5. Sentence Stems

Provide sentence stems such as the following for students to complete independently:

- A good thing about being my gender is …
- A difficult thing about being my gender is …
- It's all right for boys but not girls to …
- It's all right for girls but not boys to …
- Boys are …
- Girls are …
- Sexism means …

Once completed, students can share their responses and discuss whether the statements are true for all, most, or some boys and girls.

6. Blue Books, Pink Books

Many picture books challenge gender stereotypes. After reading aloud an appropriate book (see list), discuss: "Does the book tell the truth about some boys and some girls? What problem did the character have? If the character of the book were to become a member of the class, how would he [or she] be treated? How might the story be different if the genders of the characters were reversed?"

> **Books That Challenge Gender Stereotypes**
>
> *Picture Books*
> Browne, Anthony. *Piggybook.*
> Cole, Babette. *Princess Smartypants.* (Also: *Prince Cinders*)
> DePaola, Tomie. *Oliver Button Is a Sissy.*
> Harper, Charise Mericle. *Pink Me Up!*
> Kilodavis, Cheryl. *My Princess Boy.*
> Mackall, Dandi Daley (Illus. Renne Graef). *A Girl Named Dan.*
> McQuinn, Anna. *Lola Loves Stories.*
> Munsch, Robert. *The Paper Bag Princess.*
> Rickards, Lynne (Illus. Margaret Chamberlain). *Pink.*
> Zolotow, Charlotte (Illus. William Pene Du Bois). *William's Doll.*
>
> *Novels*
> Clements, Andrew. *Extra Credit.*
> Ellis, Deborah. *The Breadwinner* (Trilogy)
> Fine, Anne. *Bill's New Frock.*
> Fitzhugh, Louise. *Nobody's Family Is Going to Change.*
> Howe, James. *Totally Joe.*
> Murdock, Catherine Gilbert. *Dairy Queen* (Trilogy).
> Walliams, David. *The Boy in the Dress.*

Addressing Gender Equity Issues to Foster Inclusive Environments

by Mary Reid

Mary Reid is an Initial Teacher instructor at the Ontario Institute for Studies in Education, University of Toronto. She is currently conducting doctoral research focused on how teacher candidates develop effective mathematics teaching skills. Mary is a proud "dance mom" of two incredible daughters.

Building inclusive classrooms must involve deepening students' understanding of gender identity and gender stereotypes. Decades of research demonstrate that without the explicit teaching of gender equity in classrooms, it is likely that children will uphold and endorse a strict adherence to stereotypical gender roles through peer pressure and bullying. For example, students may exclude classmates based on their gender or make fun of peers who violate gender norms. Consequently, students who exhibit atypical gender behaviors often suffer from low self-esteem and low social acceptance. Given these issues, it is vital that teachers foster classroom environments in which students accept and appreciate nonconforming gender conduct, actively challenge discriminatory behaviors, and feel safe to reveal their authentic gender identity.

A research project that involved the Ontario Institute for Studies in Education/University of Toronto (OISE/UT) and a partner school provided a context for investigating issues of gender identity and stereotypes. Participants in the research study included an OISE/UT teacher candidate, an associate teacher, and 20 Grade 2 students. The associate teacher and the teacher candidate worked in partnership with two OISE/UT research coordinators to develop lessons of social justice that focused on gender issues. The goals of this project were to deepen children's understanding of gender equity concerns and to foster inclusive environments of respect, open-mindedness, and understanding of individual differences. Lamb, Bigler, Liben, and Green (2009) explain that "children's internalization of the notion that they can and should express support in public for their peers' rights to engage in non-traditional behavior can create climate of tolerance for individual differences in gender role behavior" (p. 379).

The lessons developed during this project used a diverse collection of rich literature and media texts to examine students' gender role attitudes and behaviors. Students responded to the various literature and media texts through discussion (e.g., positive problem-solving), drama (e.g., empathetic role-playing), writing (e.g., critical questions and graphic organizers), and visual arts (e.g., creation of a quilt). Students were introduced to concepts of sexism, gender stereotyping, and forms of gender-role bullying. Specifically, lessons were aimed at teaching children explicit strategies to challenge exclusion of students based on gender (e.g., a group of boys not allowing girls to play basketball at recess); lessons also focused on how to challenge teasing of children not conforming to gender norms (e.g., laughing at a boy who plays with dolls).

Diagnostic data revealed the existence of peer pressure among the Grade 2 students to adhere to gender stereotypes. Before reading the picture book *William's Doll*, students were engaged in a discussion about who can play with dolls. Following is an excerpt from that discussion:

MALE STUDENT A: No! If a boy plays with girls' dolls then they [others] will think he dresses like a girl.
MALE STUDENT B: If a boy plays with a girl's doll and a girl sees him, he might be embarrassed. That's not good.
MALE STUDENT C: Others will laugh at him.
MALE STUDENT A: And some girls play with boy dolls.
FEMALE STUDENT: My baby brother plays with girls' dolls.
TEACHER: Is that okay?

FEMALE STUDENT: Yes! (*shouts*)

MALE STUDENT B: If the boy is babies, it's okay because they don't know.

FEMALE STUDENT: Yeah, babies don't know anything, so it's okay.

As gender equity lessons were implemented daily during the teacher candidate's four-week practicum, assessment of students' responses demonstrated a growing depth of understanding of gender equity issues. Specifically, the children began to identify gender inequities and articulated how to challenge insensitive comments and actions. Midway through the practicum, the teacher candidate reflected on her students' increasing awareness of gender identity, gender stereotyping and pressures to conform to gender norms. The following is an excerpt from her journal:

> The children are becoming more empathetic and sensitive to gender issues. In today's class, the boys agreed that it's okay to play with toys like dolls, skipping ropes, and dress up. They said that they wouldn't laugh if they saw their male friends playing with such toys. More importantly, the class expressed if they saw others making fun of people because of their toys, they would tell them to stop—that's unkind.

By the end of the unit, the Grade 2 students had gained an understanding of fairness in terms of gender equity. The children began to "identify themselves as critical thinkers and in some cases, activists, which cultivated a stronger community within their classroom." The following work samples demonstrate students' culminating reflections about sexism. Most responses revealed a development of empathy and sensitivity, as students wrote about accepting gender atypical behaviors. This development certainly supported community building and provided a sense of inclusion among the students.

A published report of this project appears in a journal on research:

Reid, Mary, and Larry Swartz. 2011. "One Book, Two Books, Pink Books, Blue Books: Gender Issues for Primary Learners." In *Inquiry into Practice: Reaching Every Student Through Inclusive Curriculum Practices,* edited by Carol Rolheiser, Mark Evans, and Mira Gambhir (pp. 72–80). Toronto: Ontario Institute for Studies in Education/University of Toronto.

In closing, this research project provided evidence that the explicit teaching of gender equity issues enabled students to critically question stereotypic beliefs and assumptions. The students expressed acceptance of individual differences, particularly for atypical gender behaviors. As they considered diversity in gender identity and social justice issues connected to gender equity, both the associate teacher and the teacher candidate expressed how vital it was to pay attention to students' voices. Without a doubt, with ongoing deliberate teaching strategies that acknowledge and celebrate diversity, students become part of a caring and nurturing community of learners.

Reference:

Lamb, Lindsay M., Rebecca S. Bigler, Lynn S. Liben, and Vanessa A. Green. 2009. "Teaching Children to Confront Peers' Sexist Remarks: Implications for Theories of Gender Development and Educational Practices." *Sex Roles*, 61, 361.

Towards the Reclaiming of Aboriginal Education

by Tanya Senk

Tanya Senk, a Cree/Métis educator, is the coordinator of Aboriginal Education with the Toronto District School Board, Aboriginal Education Centre. With 15 years of experience, she demonstrates a deep interest in and commitment to equity, social justice, and community-based education. She has served as a classroom practitioner and as a course director in teacher education at York University. Examining and exploring issues of diversity through the arts is a special interest.

Educators of Aboriginal (First Nations, Métis, and Inuit) students face the daunting task of collaboratively working to recuperate, maintain, and strengthen diverse Aboriginal cultures and languages. They and the educational institutions they represent must meet the challenges that stem from the historical and contemporary relationships between Aboriginal cultures and mainstream educational systems: these include colonization and the need to adopt anti-racist or anti-oppressive stances.

Learning as a Community Activity

First Nations, Métis, and Inuit ways of knowing, situated in holistic lifelong-learning models inherently connected to community well-being, help identify what learning success means for Aboriginal students and communities. Their approach to lifelong learning moves well beyond what can be defined as "formal" education. This approach encourages community participation to draw connections to broader determinants of learning success and opens up new paths for further community involvement. It is important that First Nations, Métis, and Inuit students and their families feel welcome in schools. They need to see themselves and their cultures reflected in the curriculum and the school community.

Aboriginal peoples see learning as much more than an individual pursuit. Learning supports relationships between the individual, the family, and the community. The individual is not separated from his or her contribution to the well-being of the broader community. A sense of connection to the community strengthens the community and promotes social capital. Learning is a community activity—a process in which educators, families, Elders or Métis Senators, and community all have a role and a responsibility.

Character Education from Aboriginal Perspectives

Through this model of inclusive education as being situated in community, a special project took shape. It was connected to York University's School and Community Engaged Education initiative that took place at various schools. The primary goals of the project were to work on staff development, community and parent engagement, and knowledge mobilization, and support teachers in their knowledge and understanding of inclusive practices. The project sought to develop local community-informed, community-engaged curriculum. Inclusive Learning Communities (made up of educators, parents/guardians, community members, and organizations) were created.

During one gathering dedicated to the topic of how to create Aboriginal infused–curriculum and environments, a parent opened up a discussion on character education, commenting on how there appeared to be a lack of Aboriginal perspective(s). It was noted that the traditional Anishnawbe teachings—The Seven Grandfather Teachings—were not visibly present. These teachings are traditional teachings to know about what is important in order to live a good life. Given by Creator, they encompass respect, courage, love, humility, honesty, wisdom, and truth. Each Grandfather Teaching is a lesson considered as a gift of knowledge; all of the teachings are interconnected.

A discussion about worldviews, values, identity, relationships, holistic approaches, ideas of connectedness, and community ensued. Not long after, a school-wide, arts-based project that involved teachers, artists, parents, and community took shape. A mural was

The Seven Grandfather Teachings

To cherish knowledge is to know wisdom.

To know Love is to know peace.

To honour all of Creation is to have respect.

Bravery is to face the foe with integrity.

Honesty in facing a situation is to be brave.

Humility is to know yourself as a sacred part of Creation.

Truth is to know all of these things.

created. It was then celebrated at the National Aboriginal Day Assembly with student performances that infused Aboriginal perspectives throughout.

It was clear that the Inclusive Learning Communities provided a forum for teachers, parent/guardians, and community members to actively participate in co-constructing curriculum as it relates to the issues and considerations of community engagement at their respective school sites. The collaborative endeavors of all contributed to a transformative educational experience.

An Exploration of Culturally Responsive and Relevant Pedagogy

Throughout the project, culturally responsive and relevant pedagogy was explored as a framework in providing opportunities for educators and students to engage with inclusive and culturally relevant curricular and pedagogical practices. Building on the work of the project, in which I collaboratively participated for more than three years, I have had time to reflect upon the possibilities, challenges, and limitations of culturally responsive and relevant pedagogy in education. These opportunities have created spaces of possibility for further learning and inquiry.

What became increasingly clear through our collaborative endeavors is that culturally responsive and relevant pedagogy alone cannot address the larger social, economic, and political factors that are having an impact on Aboriginal education today. It is essential to expose and challenge racism and other forms of oppression as key barriers to achieving equity and educational decolonization.

What I have learned is that, as educators, we must confront our own complicity and culpability in the continuing structures of inequality and injustice. Despite the current discourse about the need to further develop inclusive, culturally relevant, and responsive curricular and pedagogical practices to meet the needs of marginalized, vulnerable, and racialized students, Aboriginal perspectives are still often dismissed, ignored, and unacknowledged. Culturally proficient, respectful, and relevant pedagogy and curriculum empower students to have a voice and challenge the status quo. This approach promotes the reclaiming of Aboriginal education and fosters sovereignty, self-determination, and autonomy in the hands of Aboriginal peoples. There is a great need for educators and policy makers to be more knowledgeable about and sensitive to Aboriginal cultures and histories, in order to create welcoming and inclusive schools: schools that will further promote understanding of Aboriginal peoples within society and increase Aboriginal student success and well-being as a whole.

Anti-racist Education

Without addressing racism, it is difficult to transform power relations. The inclusion of Aboriginal content and perspectives in the curriculum is crucial in recognizing and creating social justice for Aboriginal students and communities. The importance of learning about and recognizing colonization is a key element in creating spaces that foster safe and caring learning environments that nurture Aboriginal student success and well-being.

A commitment to anti-racist education was made through the internal and external partnerships of the project. Coalitions and alliances were formed within and across the diversity of Aboriginal and non-Aboriginal peoples working together to address Aboriginal student success and well-being in a common search for social justice.

Aboriginal education is not just for Aboriginal students. When non-Aboriginal students learn about the rich histories, cultures, and contemporary lives of diverse Aboriginal peoples, cross-cultural coalitions and alliances are more likely to take shape. Non-Aboriginal students learn about themselves in relationship to the experiences and lives of Aboriginal peoples. These experiences potentially create possibilities for a common commitment to social justice that leads to an equitable and more inclusive society.

Throughout the project, the following framework was applied in seeking to answer some of the challenging questions around inclusive education for Aboriginal students, families, and communities.

Apply the four Rs.

1. Show respect. *Respect* the cultural knowledge, traditions, values, and activities that individuals bring with them.
2. Ensure relevance. *Relevance* occurs when respect is embedded in the curricula, instruction, and policies.
3. Strive for reciprocity. *Reciprocity* refers to the revising of relationships between student and instructor from a hierarchy to that of a relationship focused on mentorship. In this way both individuals are viewed as learners.
4. Take responsibility. *Responsibility* for change is demanded of the instructor even if the instructor is not personally disadvantaged by the barriers of the learner.

In conclusion, there must be a continued commitment to new ideas and approaches about measuring Aboriginal student success that go beyond the limitations of schooling and performance in standardized tests. This commitment, reflected in a holistic approach, must truly encompass the well-being of Aboriginal students, families, and communities.

Putting on Another's Shoes: Working with Script

We believe that the capacity to experience something from another person's perspective is directly linked to creating a caring classroom. We also believe in the human capacity to move between imagination and reality.

As drama educators, we know that drama can provide a safe haven for students to explore issues related to social justice. The metaphor of walking in someone else's shoes in order to understand another person's experience is a strategy that allows our students to imagine that person's reality and to become more empathetic. When students have opportunities to discover that other people often do not have the same access to the future that they do, they begin to understand the need to advocate for social justice on everyone's behalf.

Working with script allows students to gain confidence as they talk about the experiences of the characters they meet and embody. The overall social well-being of the class is enhanced as students work together to solve problems, think deeply about another person's point of view, investigate new ideas, explore parallel universes, speak as the characters, and discuss their reactions to the drama from their own points of view.

The script *Aisha's Dilemma* helps students to consider an imagined, but authentic situation where a bullied student shares her feelings about the way she has been treated at school. By interpreting the scene and then improvising an ending to the scene, students can consider how they can be compassionate to those who are being ostracized. The script is provided in line master form (next page).

Aisha's Dilemma

by Kathleen Gould Lundy

MOTHER: Aisha, wake up. It is time to go to school.

AISHA: I am not feeling well. I don't want to go today.

MOTHER: But you have a test. You need to go to write the test so that you can do well. Your father and I gave up so much to bring you here. You have to go today. Besides, you will miss out on seeing your friends.

AISHA: What friends?

MOTHER: (*Putting her hand on Aisha's forehead*) Let me see if you have a temperature. No, you do not have a fever.

AISHA: Please do not make me go to school. Please. Not today and not tomorrow.

MOTHER: But you love school.

AISHA: I used to love school before we moved to this country. Now I hate every moment of it.

MOTHER: Don't say "hate." I don't like that word.

AISHA: (*under her breath*) Well, get used to it.

MOTHER: What did you say?

AISHA: Nothing.

(Aisha follows her mother into the kitchen.)

MOTHER: Why don't you tell me what is really going on?

AISHA: What?

MOTHER: Aisha—I know you. This is not like you. What is really the matter?

AISHA: You don't understand how difficult this is for me. You do not have to leave the apartment every day and go to a new place with people who don't know you.

MOTHER: I will soon. I am starting my English classes next week.

AISHA: It's not the same as when I was in school in our country. There I was smart, was a part of everything, had friends …

MOTHER: You are smart.

AISHA: *I* know that but *nobody* else does. Because I cannot speak English very well, I find it hard to get my ideas across. It sometimes is so difficult that I just shut down. And then …

MOTHER: What …?

AISHA: I can't tell you.

MOTHER: What … is it?

(Silence.)

AISHA: Yesterday … a whole bunch of kids chased me when I got off the bus. They called me names—horrible names—and made fun of my headscarf. They said things that I did not understand.

MOTHER: What? Why didn't you say something yesterday when you came home?

AISHA: I hate it here SO much!

MOTHER: Sometimes I wonder if this was the right thing to do … Coming all this way …

(Silence.)

AISHA: It was. (*Silence.*) It is. It's just hard right now.

(Silence.)

MOTHER: So, what should we do about this situation?

AISHA: I'm not sure.

(Silence.)

Pembroke Publishers © 2011 *Creating Caring Classrooms* by Kathleen Gould Lundy and Larry Swartz   ISBN 978-1-55138-270-8

Resolution of Aisha's Dilemma

1. Students work in pairs. Have them decide who is going to read Aisha's part and who is going to read the mother's part. Have them read it straight without emotion. To avoid stereotyping, advise students not to use any accents.
2. Partners reread the script, switching roles.
3. Partners decide which part they would like to play as they reread the script. Have them read the script again—this time with emotion, perhaps sadness, frustration, shock, or denial.
4. The students repeat the activity. This time as they rehearse, encourage them to include silences between the lines. What action or gesture might they add as they say their lines?
5. Prompt students to find an ending to the script.
6. As a class discuss what might happen to Aisha next. Who might she speak to? Who might the mother speak to? Students then work in pairs to improvise a scene in the future (e.g., Aisha telling the teacher, the mother going to the principal, the father getting involved, a social worker helping the family, the police being phoned).

Have the students share their various new scenes with the rest of the class, and discuss all of the possibilities, difficulties, and challenges of life in Canada for Aisha and her family. Ask: "What should people in Aisha's situation do? How can someone make sure that this kind of bullying and racism is halted?" Ask the students whether they have ever found themselves in this kind of situation. What did they do?

The next chapter naturally progresses into a discussion on confronting the bully issue.

Chapter 5

Confronting the Bully Issue

If any of you happens to see an injustice, you are no longer a spectator, you are a participant. And you have an obligation to do something.
—June Callwood

The statistics are irrefutable.

The headlines are frightening.

The stories are painful.

With the increasing severity of bullying and the accompanying media attention that bullying cases have received, parents and educators have cause to take action and ensure that bullying does not go unnoticed. In the introduction to an episode of Dr. Phil's talk show, the announcer claimed that mothers and fathers need to pay attention because 75 percent of students report that they have bullied, been bullied, or witnessed bullying incidents—and schools were not doing much about it. Interviewed that day were two young adolescent girls who had each been brutally targeted on the school bus. Both incidents were caught on videotape. Despite frequent visits from the concerned parents to school administrators, little was done to support their daughters. When asked by the interviewer, "What did the bus driver do while you were being beat up?" one girl answered, "He just kept driving the bus."

What, in fact, are schools doing to identify, understand, and confront problems with bullying? What procedures, policies, and programs are in place to acknowledge and address bullying? How do we help young people to live with integrity, civility, and compassion?

As educators, we feel a responsibility to introduce strategies that would help students come to understand those involved in the bully triangle: the bully, the bullied, and the bystander. Young people have the right to be free from teasing, harassment, and intimidation and must feel safe, secure, accepted, and valued at school. We have to both help students understand why bullies behave the way they do and recognize that students who are bullies are also capable of showing positive actions. We also need to provide students with strategies to use if they are caught in the bully web. Ultimately, our goal is to create caring classroom communities in order to help shape caring, empathetic, respectful citizens of the world.

A Matter of Relationships

Bullying, according to researcher Debra Peplar, is a relationship problem and needs relationship solutions. In our classrooms, we need to create social contexts

"You don't have to like every kid in school, but you have to honour their humanity."

—Barbara Coloroso

The Kind Campaign

Two young women, Lauren Parsekian and Molly Thompson, journeyed across America with their mothers to interview hundreds of females about girl-against-girl crimes. Every girl they talked to had an experience in becoming an aggressor or victim of gossip, competition, manipulation, jealousy, rumors, name calling, and power struggles, and ostracizing other girls. In the documentary film of their journey, titled *Finding Kind*, we witness Lauren and Molly visiting schools and uncovering girls' raw and personal stories. Lauren and Molly established the Kind campaign (www.KINDCAMPAIGN.com) with the goal of putting an end to hate and establishing a national anti-bullying school program for girls.

that promote positive interactions. We need to find space in the curriculum to help students understand that everyone has a right to respect. We also need to introduce stories in the media, in novels, picture books, films, YouTube selections, and poems that invite written, oral, and dramatic response so that students can make connections and consider strategies for dealing with troublesome situations. In our schools, our homes, and our communities, we need to help students learn to interact effectively and peacefully with one another and the world at large. We need to help all stakeholders confront the bully issue.

Despite shelves and shelves of documents, resources, and programs for educators to address prevention, conflict resolution, and peer mediation, bullying persists. It takes place from preschool through middle school through secondary school inside and outside school walls, through face-to-face interactions and through online tormenting.

As educators we face no easy task. It is easy to point fingers, place blame, fortress our schools, mandate a bully awareness week, stiffen penalties for bullying, or ignore the problem and hope it will go away. It is more challenging—and necessary—that we, in our professional roles and as family and community members, create a safe harbor for all our children. There are no simple solutions to change behaviors, and yet it is important that our students be carefully taught.

Behavior expert Barbara Coloroso informs us that people have got to be taught to discern what is right and to act on what they know is right. When we ill treat somebody we think is contemptible, it's because we've been taught that way. Bullying is a learned behavior. It can be discussed—and it can be changed. To help parents and teachers understand what they might do to teach young people to think and act ethically, Barbara Coloroso often concludes her presentations by sharing how a Holocaust survivor responded to the question of what might have been done to prevent the atrocities:

One: Pay attention.
Two: Get involved.
Three: Never look away.
    It matters.

We need to give students the tools to be able to stand up for their own rights while respecting the rights and legitimate needs of others, to handle conflicts non-violently, and to act with integrity when confronted with difficult situations.

Twelve Lessons That Help to Unpack Understanding of the Bully Issue

The following lessons help students to consider the complex issues of bullying. As students work through reading, writing, talk, drama, and arts activities that explore the world of the bully, the bullied, and the bystander, they can come to raise issues in the classroom that may be sensitive and challenging to discuss.

It is hoped that the enrichment of community, communication, collaboration, and compassion will serve as a groundwork for deepening students' understanding. No single lesson or series of lessons can change anyone's behavior. We need to provide a safe environment for students of any age to share their beliefs and stories about bullying. The sources and strategies offered in the following lessons are intended to promote public and private responses from the students as they work towards the important goal of confronting the bully issue.

| Summary of the 12 Lessons |

Summary of the 12 Lessons

1. A Triangle, a Square, and a Circle: Clarifying Relationships
2. What's in the Word? *Bully*
3. What Is Bullying? A Questionnaire
4. Words in Their Mouths: Graphic Comic Strip
5. The Crumple Person: Considering Feelings
6. What Should You Do? Ten Bullying Scenarios
7. What If? Discussion on How to Confront Bullying
8. The Bully, the Bullied, and the Bystander: From Still Image to Improvisation
9. Snippets of Text: An Impetus for Focusing on Bullying Dynamics
10. Cyberbullying: An Exploration of Perspectives
11. Names and Name Calling: Tableaux Responses
12. *Seesaw*: Script Development

Lesson One. A Triangle, a Square, and a Circle: Clarifying Relationships

Show students an image of a triangle, a square, and a circle, each of about the same size.

Ask the students these questions: "Which do you think is the bully? Which is the bullied? Which is the bystander?" Students discuss answers with one or two classmates. They should be prepared to give reasons for their choices.

Now, direct students to cut out the three shapes provided on "A Triangle, a Square, and a Circle," a line master (page 152). They are to create a design that they think would represent the bully issue. Shapes can overlap.

Students share their designs. Group members can look at the designs of others and discuss which shape they think represents the bully, the bullied, and the bystander.

As a quick, spontaneous alternative to this activity, provide students with a blank sheet of paper or file card and have them draw a circle, a square, and a triangle on the page. Then ask them to decide which shape represents the bully, the bullied, and the bystander. Encourage students to give reasons for their choices.

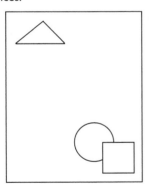

Which is the bullied? the bully? the bystander?

Extension

Students create an abstract design to represent the bully issue. They can choose to use any number of triangles, squares, or circles. Will the shapes vary in size? Will the shapes connect in any way or will they be separated? What colors would best represent the mood and feeling of the picture? Students give their art creation a title.

Note: This art activity can be done using different media (e.g., paints, markers, construction paper). The three geometric shapes can be used as a foundation for the image. How might students add lines of different lengths, thicknesses, and rhythms to create their art images?

Lesson Two. What's in the Word? *Bully*

This lesson invites students to work independently as well as to collaborate with a partner, in small groups, and as a whole class. Students work in groups to write a dictionary definition of the word *bully* using this context:

A new dictionary is about to be published, but the word *bully* has yet to be defined. As dictionary editors, you have been called upon for input.

1. To begin, students work independently. Each student is given a file card on which to write a personal definition of the word *bully* as a noun and as a verb.

2. Students in pairs exchange definitions. Ask students to consider this question: "What word or phrases from your partner's definition do you think you might like to borrow to include in a definition of *bully*?" These suggestions can be recorded on a chart.

3. Pairs work together to synthesize definitions. Encourage students to include words from each partner's definition as well as add new words.

4. Partners are then matched up with others to share definitions. Groups of four collaborate on a definition. Challenge the students by insisting that the new definition be exactly 25 words in length. Once the definitions are completed, one member of each group shares the definition with the whole class.

5. Do a shared writing activity. Students offer suggestions to create a class definition of the word *bully*. Record suggestions as offered and revise and edit as the composing process unfolds.

6. Inform students that the new dictionary will be strictly visual so that all definitions must be represented without words. Prompt students to create an image or design to represent what a bully is.

In *The Bully, the Bullied and the Bystander*, Barbara Coloroso provides the following definition: "Bullying is a conscious, willful and deliberate hostile activity intended to harm, induce fear through the threat of further aggression, and create terror" (p. 13). You might have the students consider which words from the class definition are similar to or different from Coloroso's.

With thanks to Mrs. Rachael Stein's Grade 6 class

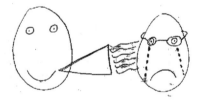

A visual definition of bullying

Definitions

> A bully is someone who thinks hurting someone is a fun thing or a good thing.   S.P.
>
> Bully—when a person comes up to you and starts to taunt you   S.V.
>
> Bullying is something that is full of non-joy, and it could lead it to something that could cost your life. T.L.
>
> A Bully is cruel, mean, strong and tough.   J.B.

Lesson Three. What Is Bullying? A Questionnaire

To prompt a discussion about bullying, students complete a questionnaire independently (see the line master next page). They then share their answers in small groups, and as a class discuss responses, stories, and issues related to bullies and victims. The discussion is framed around the following questions:

- What is a bully?
- What do you think motivates someone to behave like a bully?
- How can you prepare yourself for the possibility of encountering a bully?

Bullying: A Questionnaire

Respond to each of the following statements by checking whether you agree, feel unsure, or disagree. You will later discuss your responses in class.

	Agree	Unsure	Disagree
1. Boys usually bully more than girls do.	☐	☐	☐
2. Most bullies have friends.	☐	☐	☐
3. I can tell someone is a bully from the person's looks.	☐	☐	☐
4. Bullying is just teasing.	☐	☐	☐
5. Bullies will go away if you ignore them.	☐	☐	☐
6. Telling someone you've been bullied usually makes things worse for you.	☐	☐	☐
7. Bullying mostly happens when no one else is around.	☐	☐	☐
8. Bullies generally think badly about themselves.	☐	☐	☐
9. Once a bully, always a bully.	☐	☐	☐
10. Spreading rumors is bullying.	☐	☐	☐
11. The best way to deal with a bully is to get even.	☐	☐	☐
12. Someone who witnesses a bullying incident and does not report it is a coward.	☐	☐	☐
13. Cyberbullies will go away if no one responds to their messages.	☐	☐	☐
14. Three out of four students have been involved in bullying incidents in school.	☐	☐	☐
15. It's important to ignore bullies.	☐	☐	☐

A word to describe a bully is _____

A word to describe a target is _____

Pembroke Publishers © 2011 *Creating Caring Classrooms* by Kathleen Gould Lundy and Larry Swartz   ISBN 978-1-55138-270-8

Lesson Four. Words in Their Mouths: Graphic Comic Strip

Students examine the comic strip (see page 153 for a line master). In small groups, they can discuss what they notice. Who are the characters? What is their relationship to one another? What is the story? What scene might have preceded this story?

In groups of three, students create three tableaux images that would summarize this incident. Encourage them to pay close attention to the gestures, facial expression, and physical formation of each character in each panel.

No dialogue is provided in this comic strip. Invite the students to work independently to write verbal text inside each bubble.

Arrange students in groups of three, and have each student share ideas about what the characters are saying. Students can compare their responses. As a group, students can collaboratively write the dialogue for this comic strip.

Students next dramatize the graphic story. To begin, each student can play the part of one of the characters. The activity is then repeated so that each student will have an opportunity to role-play all parts.

Students then decide which character to play in a scene that includes this dialogue. Encourage students to consider how to say their lines to bring meaning to the text. How will they stand? sit? move? interact?

Extensions
1. Students can improvise a scene that would continue this story.
2. Students can create a one-page comic strip that continues the story.

Lesson Five. The Crumple Person: Considering Feelings

With thanks to Vanessa Russell

This lesson provides a way for students to consider the issue of name-calling and putdowns. It requires the creation of a large cut-out shape of a human body. One student can volunteer to lie down in a neutral position, with arms and legs outstretched, on a large sheet of paper while another student traces the outline of the body. This outline is then cut out. This activity might work best if students are sitting in a circle.

1. Give the cut-out human form a gender-neutral name (e.g., Chris, Pat, or Sandy). Inform students that "Chris" is not doing well today at school. Chris has been harassed and bullied, and over the week has been called a number of names that have been hurtful.
2. Prompt students to consider some of the putdown names that Chris might have heard at the school.

The nature of this activity encourages students to be trusting of each other. Some putdowns can be considered "sensitive" because of their sexual, racial, or cultural intent. Here, students are invited to volunteer these names to help them consider their meaning and intent.

3. Invite students to come up to Chris to record a putdown term that Chris might have heard. Students are given a marker to write the term somewhere on the body. As each derogatory name is added, the figure is crumpled once by the student who identified the putdown word.

4. The activity continues with volunteers coming forward. Some may choose to record more than one item. Some may choose to remain silent during the activity. It is recommended to provide wait time for students to come forward.

5. Show Chris to each student one by one and see whether anyone chooses to add a name or not.

6. Once the figure is fully crumpled, ask: "How is Chris different than before? How do you think Chris feels? How do you think Chris might act or behave?"

7. Ask students to consider how they might help Chris feel better. What could they say or do? With each suggestion, individuals come forward and smooth over any place where Chris has been harmed. The activity continues until Chris is entirely uncrumpled.

8. Ask the students: "How is Chris different from the beginning of the class? How might Chris feel now? Does Chris feel better?" Discuss how Chris's "scars" or putdowns might have a visible and lasting effect.

9. The class can discuss how to ensure that no one gets "crumpled" in the class. What are some ground rules and group norms that need to be considered? Are these realistic? Can there be consequences if rules are broken?

10. Invite students to record their feelings about the activity. How did this activity help them think about bullying behavior? How did it connect to their own experiences or to those of someone they know?

Extension

The Crumple Person lesson can be the foundation of a writing-in-role activity. Students can write a letter from the point of view of Chris, someone who bullied Chris, or a bystander who witnessed the putdowns. These letters can be exchanged, and students can improvise a meeting between two characters at some future date in Chris's life.

Variations on "The Crumple Person": Although the lesson can be considered most powerful when shared with a group sitting in a circle, other teachers have done similar activities in the following ways:

- Students work alone or in small groups to write putdowns on a character figure.
- In lieu of crumpling a student outline, students tear the cut-out figure. The scars can then be taped together.
- Nails hammered into a board can also be used. Each time a putdown is offered, students hammer a nail into a block of wood. The nails can be removed to represent "scars."

Lesson Six. What Should You Do? Ten Bullying Scenarios

The line master "What Should You Do?" presents incidents of bullying and alternatives for dealing with them. Let students study the scenarios independently and then share their responses in small groups. Encourage the students to discuss the challenges of putting each of the four possible choices into action.

What Should You Do? Alternatives for Discussion

1. A bully wants you to give him your homework. You should
   a) not give it to him—insist that he do it himself.
   b) offer to help him get it done this one time.
   c) give him your homework so he won't hurt you.
   d) tell the teacher that he wants to copy your homework.

2. You made friends with your new neighbor. Your old friends make fun of her because the coat she wears is badly torn. You should
   a) ignore your friends; say nothing.
   b) tell your friends they are being mean and should stop.
   c) tell your neighbor that it's time to buy a new coat.
   d) invite your old friends over to the house to have fun with the new neighbor.

3. You are in the playground minding your own business. An older kid trips you on purpose. You should
   a) get some friends together to scare the older kid.
   b) tell the kid to apologize.
   c) say you'll hit him if he tries it again.
   d) laugh it off; it didn't hurt much.

4. Your friends are going to a see a movie and haven't included you. You should
   a) go to the movie with someone else.
   b) offer them something so they'll invite you to go with them.
   c) choose not to speak to them again.
   d) sit down and cry.

5. You hear a good friend calling someone you don't know a bad name. You should
   a) try not to get involved.
   b) join him, but privately tell the target you don't mean it.
   c) ask your friend why she enjoys making someone feel bad.
   d) call your friend a bad name.

6. You are being bullied at school. There is a boy who punches you and takes things from your desk. Your dad tells you to hit him back. You should
   a) do what your dad says.
   b) do nothing; it will stop.
   c) tell someone else to hurt the boy.
   d) tell another adult about the problem.

7. You walk by a daycare centre every day. You see one of the caregivers being mean to a little boy you know day after day. Today you witnessed her slapping the little boy on the back when he refused to pick up his toys. You should
   a) tell the caregiver you've seen what she did and advise her to stop.
   b) tell a supervisor about what you have seen.
   c) tell the little boy to tell his parents what happened.
   d) say nothing; the boy was being naughty.

8. Your friends want to leave the schoolyard at lunchtime even though it's against the school rules. You don't want to get into trouble, but a couple of friends continue to pressure you to join them. You should
   a) go with the group—one time won't hurt.
   b) stay at school even though you may have to be alone.
   c) look for a new group of friends: following the school rules is important.
   d) tell a school staff member about your friends.

9. A friend has told you that she is being sexually harassed. She doesn't want to tell her parents because, she says, she'll get into trouble. You should
   a) advise your friend to go to a trusted adult to tell what's happening.
   b) give your friend strategies on how to ignore the bully (e.g., stick with friends, avoid being alone with him).
   c) offer to talk to the bully (with or without her).
   d) tell someone else you know about the incident because you don't know how to handle it.

10. Stan always brags about the pranks he pulls. You've never seen any and think that Stan just makes up these stories. One day, you notice that someone's locker has been damaged. There is a rumor that Stan is responsible. You should
   a) take Stan's side and convince others that he didn't do it.
   b) spread a rumor that someone else did it.
   c) talk to Stan; tell him to confess that he's been lying about all his pranks.
   d) find out who started the rumor and ask how they know it's true.

Pembroke Publishers © 2011 Creating Caring Classrooms by Kathleen Gould Lundy and Larry Swartz   ISBN 978-1-55138-270-8

Lesson Seven. What If? Discussion on How to Confront Bullying

To begin, offer just one bullying scenario to the whole class to discuss. Some students may choose to reveal similar incidents that have happened to them. As the discussion continues, have students offer suggestions about how to handle the situation in the present and for the future.

The following strategies can be used to prepare lessons with "What if?" scenarios. (See the line master on the next page.)

- *Written responses:* Distribute the line master to the class. Students can review the list and then choose one situation to focus on. To answer the "What if" question, they can write a possible solution to the problem, meet with others who have chosen the same scenario, and discuss solutions to the problem.

- *Small-group discussion:* The "What if" statements can be cut into strips and placed in an envelope. Students working pairs or small groups can select one item from the envelope to discuss. Groups can be matched up, with each group presenting the problem and possible solutions.

- *Role-playing:* Students form groups of two or three. Each group is assigned a scenario. The group discusses the incident and possible solutions. The group then develops a short scene. Once the students have rehearsed the scene, they can present it to another group that discusses some ways to handle the problem.

Lesson Eight. The Bully, the Bullied, and the Bystander: From Still Image to Improvisation

Patricia Polacco's autobiographical book tells the story of a Grade 5 girl, little Trisha, who can't seem to read. A new teacher, Mr. Falker, recognizes Trisha's troubles and helps to uncover the artistic talents within. He also confronts the class when they make fun of Trisha: "Stop! Are all of you so perfect that you can look at another person and find fault with her?" In this lesson, students represent the bully, the bullied, and the bystander.

Part A
1. Provide students with the image (next page) projected on the overhead projector or the SMART Board.
2. Hand each student an index card. Have them write at the top of the card the words *I see …* In the middle of the card, have them write *I remember …* Near the bottom of the card, have them write *I imagine …*
3. Give students about five minutes to write about what they see in the illustration. What does the image remind them of in their personal lives or that of someone they know? What do they imagine might be happening in the picture?
4. Ask students to find a partner and share what they have written; then, have them talk to other partners or to the whole class about the image and their response. Here are some questions for discussion:

- What feelings do they have about this girl?
- What do they think has happened to this girl moments before? days before?
- What should the girl in the picture do?
- Who is *not* seen in this picture? What other characters might be included in it?

5. Draw a large human figure on the chalkboard. Write the word *Trisha* on the inside of the figure.

- Have students think of how Trisha is feeling and what she is thinking. Invite them to come up to the chalkboard and write these words inside the figure outline.

From *Thank You, Mr. Falker* by Patricia Polacco, Copyright c 1998 by Babushka, Inc. Used by permission of Philomel Books, A Division of Penguin Young Readers Group. All rights reserved.

What if ...?

The incidents outlined below are intended to prompt discussion about how students would respond to various situations. They focus on the challenges of dealing with bullying incidents past, present, and future.

1. *What if* you were walking down the hall of your school and someone called you a bad name?
2. *What if* you become aware of someone spreading a nasty rumor about your brother or sister?
3. *What if* you received an email that said something bad about one of your best friends?
4. *What if* one of your teachers keeps picking on a classmate? It's true the classmate is not paying attention or often forgets his homework, but the teacher shouts at him and gives him trouble.
5. *What if* you witness someone spray-painting a horrible message on the wall outside your school?
6. *What if* someone in the cafeteria makes rude comments about a classmate who is overweight?
7. *What if* you overhear a racist comment about another person who registered as a new student at the school the same time as you?
8. *What if* someone in your class expresses dismay that their iPod has disappeared? You have seen it in another student's locker. The person is a stranger to you.
9. *What if* you find a threatening note on your desk when you walk into the classroom?
10. *What if* you were in a restaurant and heard a customer making fun of the waitress's accent?
11. *What if* a kid older than you starts making fun of you, calling you poor because of the street you live on? You were minding your own business. You are on the bus and are not allowed to move seats. You know that others have been in a similar situation.
12. *What if* your friend shoplifts something and then brags about it to you? You are both in the mall. To deter you from telling, she threatens to say that you and she planned to steal the item together.
13. *What if* your older brother or sister grabs the remote control and changes the channel even though you were watching your favorite program? No adult is at home.
14. *What if*, on the subway with your friend, you hear some kids from your school saying rude things about your friend. You know that your friend's mother has advised her to ignore such incidents.
15. *What if* you receive a rude text message from someone you don't know? You ignore it, but over the month, the messages get worse.
16. *What if* you really want to join a group of kids you think are cool, but they reject you?
17. *What if* someone in the next grade pushes you into a locker but says, "Sorry"? You hear giggling as that person walks away from you.
18. *What if* a guy at school says "fag" every time he passes you in the hallway?

Pembroke Publishers © 2011 *Creating Caring Classrooms* by Kathleen Gould Lundy and Larry Swartz   ISBN 978-1-55138-270-8

- Prompt students to write words that describe the pressures that Trisha must be feeling on the outside of the figure.
- Around the figure, have students record the names of people to whom Trisha turns to for help and support.

Part B

The illustration used in the activity above provides an image of someone who has been bullied. What we don't see in the picture are people clearly in the bully and bystander roles. The following activity will have students role-play the part of a targeted person like Trisha and come to better understand the feelings, attitudes, and problems of people in similar situations.

1. Students are directed to use their bodies to create a statue titled "The Bully." Once each person has made a still image independently and frozen into a position, draw everyone's attention to the hand gestures represented (e.g., arms folded, fists, pointed fingers). Ask them to consider what the message behind each gesture is. Does the hand gesture imply that a physical abuse is intended to take place?

2. Students create a statue titled "The Target." Once each person has made a still image, draw their attention to the way the head has been placed. How do these images differ from the bully images? (They likely include hands in front of face, lowered head, and scared look.) What is the message behind each of these images?

3. Divide the group in half. Group 1 re-creates the bully statue, while group 2 watches. What do they notice about the bully images?

4. Group 2 then re-creates the victim/target statues while group 1 watches. What do they notice about these images?

5. Group 1 re-creates the bully statue one more time. Tell each person in group 2 to match up with a member of group 1 to create a new tableau featuring two people.

6. Invite students to consider what their characters are thinking at that very moment. Tap the shoulder of each participant as a cue for each person to call out what the character he or she has become is thinking. Tell students they might be called upon more than once. They can repeat a line or come up with a new line.

7. Tell the students to re-create their tableaux images. This time the scene is brought to life. Students can improvise conversation from their own character's point of view. The goal of this activity is to spontaneously respond to what each of the characters says.

It is important to remind the students that the bully and the target are not allowed to touch each other at this point. Challenge the students to stay in role for one minute.

8. On a signal, have students switch roles, so the bully becomes the target. Pairs can begin by re-creating the still image. Students can use some of the conversation from the previous improvisation, but they are not required to repeat the exact same conversation. Challenge the students to stay in role for 90 seconds.

9. Partners return to their original role and repeat the improvisation. Advise students that you will not assign a time limit. Provide this challenge: "Can the victim persuade the bully to stop the behavior? What arguments will you give?"

10. Have the targets stand in front of the bully characters. As teacher, interview the targets to determine what took place. Ask questions such as these: "Why is this person picking on you? Do you think this bully targets other people? What was the most hurtful thing the bully said to you? What did you do or say to persuade the bully to stop? Do you think you could ever be friends with this person? Are you going to tell others about this incident?"

Extensions

1. Students can work with their partners to create a new scene that might take place later that day or week. Those students who were the bully character now become the target they tormented. Those who were the target now become someone the target might turn to (e.g., a sibling, a best friend, an employer, a neighbor, a social worker, or a police officer). The goal of this improvisation is

- to have the target tell what happened
- to offer solutions about what might be done to deal with the bully

After the improvisation, survey the students to find out what kind of advice (if any) was given to the target. The class can discuss strategies that a target might take to prepare for meeting a bully, for dealing with the bully.

2. Students can work in groups of three. One person is a bully, one is the bullied, and one is the bystander. The bystander is an eyewitness to the bully scene. What will he or she report to the authorities (played by the teacher in role)? The trio can switch roles. The challenge is for the bystander to intervene. What might be said to the bully and the target to stop this bullying incident?

Lesson Nine. Snippets of Text: An Impetus for Focusing on Bullying Dynamics

The snippets featured on the "Bully Snippets" line masters (pages 131 and 132) are suitable sources for interpreting as well as improvising text. These snippets come from a number of poems that have been gathered from a wide range of resources on the bully issue (see Appendix A). Various snippets touch on the roles of the bully, the bullied, and the bystander.

This exercise allows students to play with language in the various "bubbles" and to literally "see" how bullying occurs, how power dynamics play out, and what kinds of interventions could be done to stop or lessen this kind of behavior. There needs to be some time set aside for the discussion and the unpacking of these scenes—sharing of personal stories and envisioning strategies that the victim and the bystander need to be equipped with to confront these situations and make positive changes in bully behavior.

How to Make an Entrance

There's more than one way to create the group sculpture. Students can enter making the gesture only. Once all participants have entered the scene, each individual, in turn, says his or her line and creates a new gesture. You can let the students decide the most effective way to enter the scene. Adding music, props, or masks can enhance the theatrical presentation.

1. Students can either randomly select a bully snippet or be assigned a snippet while sitting in a circle. Once students have a focus snippet, they can practise ways to read it aloud (e.g., whispering, shouting, with anger, with fear, questioning). Tell students to establish eye contact with someone across the circle and say the line to them. They can do this a few times.

2. In a circle, one at a time, students read their line of text out loud. Ask them how they think the character might give this line. Continue until all snippets are read.

3. Repeat the readings in one or more of the following ways. Students may need the security of reading the text from the page; however, through repeated activities, they should become familiar with the text:

- Students stand as they say their line.
- Students add a gesture before or after saying their line.
- Students add a gesture and are invited to freeze their action.
- Each student, in turn, shares a gesture only and freezes the position (no verbal text).
- Students rearrange themselves in the circle. Students read their line, add a gesture, and freeze.

4. Invite students to make a group sculpture using the snippets. Each student enters the space in the circle and says his or her line, adding a gesture before or after the line. Have students create a still image right after they've said their line. As someone enters the circle, he or she can choose a space to perform, perhaps making some kind of attachment to a person already inside the circle. The activity continues until everyone has recited a line. One option is for students to repeat the final line and create a new, final still image.

Improvising from Bully Snippets

An alternative or extension to interpreting bully snippets is to use them as the basis for improvisation. Here is a procedure.

1. Have each student consider whether their snippet is told from the point of view of a bully, a bullied person, or a bystander. Why might someone say this? Students can share their responses in small groups.
2. Randomly assign students to work in pairs. Prompt the students to create a still image with two characters. Once each pair is satisfied with its tableau, participants say the lines of text out loud.
3. Invite students to become the characters who might say these lines. Encourage them to imagine what happened for that person to have this thought. Partners can take turns to tell their stories in role. As the conversation continues, encourage students to ask questions to uncover the story and find out the person's feelings about what happened.
4. Students now work in groups of four. Each person introduces his or her partner by retelling the story just heard. (Partner A tells partner B's story; partner B tells partner A's story.)
5. Groups of four can create a tableau that would show each of these characters. Challenge the students to come up with a *new* line of snippet text that represents something this character might say or how this character might feel.

Options for further exploration

1. Students can use the snippet that has been assigned to them (or another snippet featured on the page). Invite them to add a thought to this snippet, perhaps an idea before the snippet, after the snippet, or before and after the snippet.
2. Students can share their work with a partner. Invite students to create a free-verse poem by rearranging their words randomly on the page. In free-verse poetry, the number of words on a single line can vary. Students can play with the white spaces to complete a poem.
3. Students can read their new poems out loud as short monologues about a bully, bullied, or bystander.
4. Students can create a graffiti wall of bully snippets. The graffiti wall can be created using words, visual images, or a combination of both.

Lesson Ten. Cyberbullying Scenario: An Exploration of Perspectives

Students assemble in groups of five, and one person volunteers to be given the first bit of information. Volunteers are pulled aside and given the information on Samara's father, perhaps on file cards.

Bully Snippets — Thought

I wished I hadn't joined in.

I hope his mother loved him.

Remember me? I am the boy who sought friendship.

Inside she knows how she made you feel.

One day
Like the snap of a finger
She stopped liking me.

A rock drops in my gut.

I was eight years old
And I was in his power

If I asked him home for dinner
I wonder if he'd come.

It's hard to fit in with these girls.
I see them whispering in the hall.

Her words are scalpels,
Cutting self-esteem.

Cuts and bruises now have healed.
It's words that I remember.

Do all the good you can
By all the means you can.

Thank you bullies that built me
With all of your crumbling hate.

Forgiveness touched me like a sea.

This vest I'm wearing is wordproof.

Life doesn't frighten me at all.

Kids shouting, kids staring
All this torture I'm bearing.

I can light candles in my mind.

I cannot hide. It hurts inside.

Pembroke Publishers © 2011 *Creating Caring Classrooms* by Kathleen Gould Lundy and Larry Swartz   ISBN 978-1-55138-270-8

Bully Snippets — Speech

Blubber Lips, Blubber Lips
Here comes Blubber Lips!

Hey, Rabbit, whatchya doin?

Life doesn't frighten me at all.

Strong as a bear
Tough
Never afraid for one second.

Don't get your pleasure from my pain.

Hey you, c'mere!!!

I do not like the company you keep.

A cat's a wonderful creature
That does not converse with its fleas.

You wouldn't know it by looking at him.

You can't come onto our street.

I have feelings just like you!

One day like the snap of a finger, she stopped liking me.

Will you chase my fears away?

Remember me? I'm the boy who sought friendship.

Pembroke Publishers © 2011 *Creating Caring Classrooms* by Kathleen Gould Lundy and Larry Swartz   ISBN 978-1-55138-270-8

Phase One: A Father's Dilemma

Samara's Father

I can't stand hearing that she is afraid to go to school. You would think that after all I have taught her about standing up for herself, she would not be in this position now. She has everything she needs—her own room, a cell phone, her own computer for goodness sake. What else could a kid want?

Give these instructions to the volunteers: "Assume that the members of your group are going to be playing people who are interested in what you have to say. When you return to the group, adopt the role of Samara's father. Don't read the snippet to the group members, but say what he would say in your own words."

Volunteers review the snippet while remaining group members are given the following information: "The volunteer who has left your group is going to return in a few minutes. I have instructed that student to adopt a role and speak in role. I am not going to tell you how to respond except to say that you must listen to this person and ask further questions about his predicament. See how much you can find out about this person's story."

Volunteers return to their groups, and time is given to conduct an interview. Typically, the students are very engaged with the task. In order to assess the involvement of group members, stop the role-playing and randomly ask members of various groups to stand and say what they have learned about Samara's father's story as the following shows:

"It seems that he has a daughter named Samara who appears to be having some difficulty at school."

"The father is very frustrated by his daughter."

"He feels that he has given her everything and that she will not stand up for herself."

Phase Two: A Mother's Dilemma

New volunteers are called over to the side of the room and given new information.

Samara's Mother

Samara won't let me call the school. She says that it will just make it worse. I can't stand seeing her this way. She used to be such a happy child. Since she has gone to that new school, things are very different for her. She is so sad all of the time. It does not matter where she is—home, school, at her grandparents', anywhere. She is always quiet and … just sad. Nothing I do or say seems to do any good.

Volunteers return to their groups to work in role. The interviewing exercise is repeated, and the mother and father are allowed to interact as well as answer questions from the group members.

The role-playing concludes. On a signal, each group re-plays part of the conversation so the rest of the class can hear it. This technique, Overheard Conversations, is another formative assessment tool to see how engaged the students are with the task and what they are saying to one another in role. Here is an example of what has been "played back" to a class:

FATHER: The problem as I see it is that you have always been too protective of the girl. That is why she is in this mess.

MOTHER: That is unfair. You always blame me when it comes to the difficult things in life.

STUDENT QUESTIONER: Could we get back to talking about Samara and what we can do to make her feel that she can return to school?

Phase Three: The Onlooker's Dilemma

When some time has passed, a third volunteer from each group comes over to the side of the room. This person is given the same information as was given to the mother and the father. The "Jodies" are directed to invent the story of what happened last term.

> **Jodie—Onlooker**
>
> I know that I should do something about what is happening to Samara, but I have my own difficulties at the moment. I know these kids. They would just turn on me if I interfered and I don't need that after what happened to me last term in this class.

After the role-playing has gone on for some time, ask the Jodies to stand and tell the story of their own bullying situation. They speak in role and answer any questions: "What are your feelings about the situation? What is preventing you from getting involved? What are you going to do next?"

Phase Four: The Counsellor's Support

A fourth volunteer is assigned to play the role of Samara, and the fifth volunteer is assigned to play the role of a student social worker doing her first family counselling session.

For this interview, fathers, mothers, and Jodies sit behind an imaginary Plexiglas window so that they can hear everything that Samara tells the social worker, but cannot intervene.

> **Samara**
>
> What nobody understands is that I can't even get away from them when I get home. They are everywhere. I can't be on my computer because somehow they have figured out my password. They even text-message me. I have not told any of this to Mom or Dad. They would freak and take away my phone. I need it in case something bad happens.

Phase Five: Writing in Role

For the summative evaluation, students write in role.

- The social workers write clinical reports of what they discovered when they interviewed Samara. They need to date and sign their reports.
- The Samaras write in their diaries and begin their writing in role with "Dear Diary …"
- The mothers and fathers write letters to their daughter in response to what they heard her say to the social worker.
- The Jodies write victim impact statements about how the bullying in the school has affected them.

Once all group members complete their writing, students are positioned one group at a time in the centre of the classroom space. The Samaras sit on chairs and the Jodies sit at their feet. The social workers stand beside them, and the parents form a larger circle right by their daughter. As the orchestra leader, the teacher gives these directions:

When I touch you on the shoulder, I want you to begin reading your writing. As soon as you hear another person reading, you stop and listen to the next voice. If I touch your shoulder again, it means that I want you to continue reading from where you left off. In this way, we will be creating a combination of viewpoints and voices that will tell Samara's story in a theatrical, moving way.

Here is part of a transcript of what took place in one class:

SAMARA: Dear diary, I cannot tell you how wonderful it was to finally tell someone about my problems.
SOCIAL WORKER: October 26. I met with Samara today at lunch. She seemed to be in quite a bit of distress …
SAMARA: Dear diary, I was worried about telling the social worker about what has been happening to me for the past nine months of my life.
JODY: I tell the court what it has been like to live in fear of being laughed at 24/7.
MOTHER: My darling Samara, how could we have ever known that you were being tormented in this way?
SAMARA: Dear diary, At last I feel that I can breathe.
JODY: I tell the court that bullying is something that eats away at your soul.
FATHER: Dear Samara: I have been insensitive and wrong, and I want to tell you how sorry I am for the way that I treated you …

Lesson Eleven. Names and Name Calling: Tableaux Responses

This lesson is based on using a picture book, *The Name Jar* by Yangsook Choi. Before the class works with the book, it is recommended that they do a few name-related activities, outlined below.

- ### *Name Call: Game*
Students go around the circle. On a signal, each student says aloud his or her name. The activity is repeated, this time with the rest of the class repeating each name as it is given. Once more the game is played with each student saying his or her name and accompanying it by a gesture. The group repeats the name and the gesture. Each student has a turn.

- ### *What's in a Name?—Personal Stories*
Have the students find a partner and tell them the story of their name. If they don't have a particular story, ask them to tell a name story about someone they know or someone in their family. (See page 21.) Two groups join together. Each person tells the new partners the first partner's name story. Students then assemble as a class and students share interesting stories they heard.

1. Once students have engaged in these activities, it is time to introduce *The Name Jar* through a teacher read-aloud. The book tells the story about a little girl with a special name, but things begin to go bad for her because the students have trouble pronouncing it. It is suggested that just the beginning of the story, until the students get off the bus, be read.
2. Working in small groups, students represent through a tableau what happened on the bus. Once their still images are completed, students share them with others. Ask the students these questions: "What words would describe Unhei's situation? What was Unhei thinking and feeling? How do we know? What is the tension or problem in this scene?"

See the Spotlight on the Classroom titled "The Shine Project: Communication, Collaboration, and Compassion Meet in an Arts-Based Project" by Raymond Peart for information related to this lesson.

Writing in Role as Unhei's Korean Friends

Dear Unhei:

… We visited your grandma and she talked about you! She misses you. In fact, she is worried sick about you. She seemed very upset and almost cried. This made us very worried about you. Is there anything we can do to make you feel better? Are you being bullied in school? Are you hurting inside? Is anyone being mean to you or bothering you? …

You can be open with us no matter what. Our love never goes away. So please tell us what's wrong. We are here for you. Call us anytime you need to. We are only a phone call away …

3. Ask all of the students who represented Unhei in tableaux to assemble in the middle of the classroom. They are to re-create the way they were positioned in their original tableaux. They can create a statue gallery that depicts Unhei's feelings and thoughts when she was being bullied on the bus. Although students are working independently, this statue gallery becomes a collective representation of the character.

Ask for student volunteers to move the characters around so that some statement of Unhei's pain and sadness can be revealed to the audience through the gallery. Students can whisper in the ear of the character and have her move into a different position in the gallery many times. There can be many interpretations and iterations of Unhei's feelings and thoughts. Encourage silence.

4. The teacher in role as Unhei's grandmother sits at the front of the classroom and calls the students together. They are representing Unhei's friends from Korea. The teacher says:

> Thank you for coming to my house today after school. I am so worried about Unhei. I receive letters from her, but she does not tell me very much about what is going on at school. Unhei loved school when she lived in Korea and spoke about it all the time. Now she never mentions it. You are her Korean friends. You know Unhei. Do you think that she is unhappy? What can we do to have her tell her story? How can we find out what is going on in her life so far away?

The students in role as Unhei's Korean friends make suggestions. If they suggest that they write Unhei a letter, encourage them to work in partners or in small groups to ask questions so that Unhei will tell her story of being made fun of because of her name. Have the students share their writing. (The writing in role at left comes from Grade 4/5 students at Shoreham Public School.)

5. If Unhei could express these feelings, what would she say? Ask students to go back into their groups and re-create their tableaux; however, this time each student playing Unhei will step out of the tableau and speak her true feelings and thoughts. Direct the group to help Unhei with her monologue. If the student playing Unhei is too shy to speak, allow another member to speak for her. (The students will have to rearrange their tableau to make this happen.)

6. Ask the class the following questions which provide a framework for having students reflect on the story and the drama.

- How difficult is it for someone like Unhei to stand up for herself?
- What made her circumstances difficult?
- Is it possible to ignore bullying like this and walk away?
- Why is that not a good idea?
- What can kids who are being bullied do?
- What can you do if you do not speak English as well as you wish?
- Why do you think people become bullies?
- Why do bystanders often do nothing?
- What should or could bystanders do?

As students share their responses about a fictional character, they can further develop an understanding of compassion.

Lesson Twelve. *Seesaw*: Script Development

The movies, television shows, and plays we see all begin with a script. Like other forms of literature, a script tells a story, but it may include information such as stage directions that reflect how actors might move to clarify the sense of the action and help turn the story into something visual for an audience to enjoy. Scripts entertain and inform us, and give the actors and directors a chance to use their imaginations to interpret a story in different ways.

The script on page 139 is one scene from the play *Seesaw* by Dennis Foon. In this scene only two characters speak. Students can explore the process of interpreting a piece of script by experimenting with ways to say the lines and present them for an audience. Encourage them to experiment with each of the roles in this script.

Ten Ways to Experiment with a Script

The following strategies are suggested ways to rehearse a script. Although the strategies apply to the scene from *Seesaw*, classes can also use them with other scripts. For purposes of rehearsal, students can change the gender of the characters, as needed.

1. Students each choose a role to read aloud. Once they are familiar with their lines, they work with others to read the script aloud.

2. Students read the script at triple speed, ensuring that each line is articulated. Actions can be included and performed quickly.

3. Between the saying aloud of each character's lines, students pause. They count three to five seconds before saying the next line. Ask them to consider what gestures and actions they could add during the pauses.

4. Each character adds an appropriate action or gesture when beginning a speech. In-role students might stand or sit, move to another space, approach another character, or perform an activity that would add meaning to the scene. Students can decide when it is important to remain still, without adding an action or gesture.

5. Students decide how to read the script aloud in order to fulfill the feelings, mood, and intentions of the dialogue. Actors can both read in a whisper or both in a loud voice (but not shouting), or one voice can be loud and one soft.

6. The characters say their lines, maintaining eye contact during the whole scene; similarly, they can say their lines without making any eye contact, back to back or spread far apart.

7. Students experiment with standing or sitting. They consider how the scene would be different if both characters were sitting or if one character stood.

8. Ignoring any stage directions, students work in partners to read the script one word at a time.

9. Students experiment with different styles to add freshness to the scene. How might they read the lines if the scene was from a western movie, a horror movie, a cartoon, or a soap opera?

10. Students record the script as a radio play. They can listen to the recording and consider what revisions might be needed to make their interpretation more effective.

1. Students put the script aside and improvise the scene. They can include some of the dialogue from the original script, change the dialogue, or add new dialogue. After the improvisation, students discuss the changes they made to the original script. (*Note:* They are only improvising here; they are not writing a script, so they don't have to record it.)

2. In pairs, students discuss what might happen next between Josh and Adam. They can then extend the script by becoming script writers and drafting new lines. Partners can add on lines of dialogue that these characters might say. They can then rehearse the new script written.

3. Ask students this question: "How might this script be different if you were to add a new character?" Students might wish to improvise the scene with a third member of the group. They can then prepare a written version of the script they have improvised.

4. Students share new scripted scenes with other groups. Invite them to consider how they might create a short play together. Have them address these questions: What scenes might come before the one by Dennis Foon? What dialogue might come immediately after this scene? later in the play? What character(s) might be added to create the short play? Students might wish to rehearse and present a collaboratively prepared play to another class in the school.

5. Find another scripted scene from the play *Seesaw* for students to interpret. Allow students to work with a different partner or in larger groups to rehearse other scenes from the play.

"Self-Reflection: Confronting the Bully Issue" (page 140) is designed to help students consider their awareness of bully incidents in their lives and how well they treat others in their classroom and school community. By completing this sheet, however, students can consider their involvement in working through the lessons that unpack bullying and their own behaviors and relationships with others.

Once they have completed the self-reflection, students can share their thoughts with a trusted friend, or confer with a teacher or adult. Students may choose to keep the answers to these statements private, and their desire for confidentiality should be respected.

A Scene from *Seesaw*

by Dennis Foon

JOSH: Hello, Adam.

ADAM: What did you call me?

JOSH: Adam.

ADAM: Did I say you could call me that?

JOSH: No.

ADAM: Then why'd you say it?

JOSH: I don't know.

ADAM: What?

JOSH: I don't know.

ADAM: What?

JOSH: I don't know.

ADAM: What?

JOSH: I don't know.

ADAM: You wanna live?

JOSH: Yes.

ADAM: Then whattaya got for me today?

(*Josh reaches into his pocket, gives Adam money.*)

ADAM: Is that all?

JOSH: Uh huh.

ADAM: Are you holding out on me?

JOSH: No.

ADAM: You better not be.

Excerpted from *Seesaw* by Dennis Foon Copyright c 1993. Reprinted by Permission of Playwrights Canada Press.

Pembroke Publishers © 2011 *Creating Caring Classrooms* by Kathleen Gould Lundy and Larry Swartz   ISBN 978-1-55138-255-5

Self-Reflection: Confronting the Bully Issue

Read each statement and think about your life in the last three to four weeks. Put a check mark in the appropriate column. Once you have completed the reflection, share your thoughts with a trusted friend, or pass this list on to your teacher.

Part A: *How I Behaved*

	Often	Once	Not Yet
I said something nice to someone	☐	☐	☐
I heard someone being called a name so I intervened	☐	☐	☐
I talked to someone about a problem he or she had	☐	☐	☐
I saw someone being bullied and I went to get help	☐	☐	☐
I tried hard to get along with others	☐	☐	☐
I changed my opinion about someone	☐	☐	☐

Part B: *How Others Treated Me*

	Yes	No
Someone made me feel bad about myself.	☐	☐
Someone made me feel good about myself.	☐	☐
Someone tried to make me do something I didn't want to do.	☐	☐
Someone helped me deal with a bullying incident.	☐	☐
Someone hurt me.	☐	☐
Someone was kind to me.		

Part C: *What I Learned*

Stories or feelings that came to mind as I completed this self-reflection:

_____

An activity that particularly helped me to better understand the bully issue:

_____

Something I learned about bullying:

_____

Advice I would give to a teacher about how to deal with bullies:

_____

If you need to, write on the back of this sheet.

Pembroke Publishers © 2011 *Creating Caring Classrooms* by Kathleen Gould Lundy and Larry Swartz   ISBN 978-1-55138-255-5

An Education in Bullying

by Miranda Lytle

Miranda is an elementary teacher living and working in southern Ontario. She recently earned her master's degree in education from Nipissing University. In her research, Miranda investigated beginning teachers' perspectives on and practices in dealing with bullying at school.

It is not unusual for classroom teachers to hear students complain of teasing, name-calling, or refusals to share or work with other students, but it is important to differentiate between bullying and inappropriate classroom behaviors. What sets bullying apart from other behaviors is the inclusion of three principal characteristics:

1. Actions are repeated over time; the bullying does not just happen once.
2. An unfair matching of participants exists. The imbalance of power may be real or perceived, for example, strength or number of bullies, higher status, or position of power.
3. The behavior is deliberate and intentional; the purpose is to cause harm or fear to another person's body, feelings, or reputation.

As classroom teachers, we are expected to be the first line of defence against bullying (Public Safety Canada 2008).

Becoming Aware of the Problem

One of my most significant experiences with bullying among students occurred in my junior classroom. Over the course of the school year, I recognized the signs of bullying among several students; the most severe situation was between Dennis and Nathan (pseudonyms are used to protect the identities of those involved). I knew that something must be done to address the ongoing bullying, as it was detrimental to the well-being of Dennis, the target, and also the greater classroom community—but where to start? Which program would engage the students and affect change in their behavior?

The bullying began as Nathan would tease Dennis for anything and everything—Dennis didn't have the right clothes, he had previously been held back a year, his home life was atypical. Nathan would taunt Dennis, encouraging other kids to laugh at his jokes. As Dennis became more and more upset, Nathan would bully him further in the hope of provoking him. In order to achieve this, Nathan would throw small items, such as erasers and pen caps, at Dennis, mimic what Dennis said, or follow his classmate around. This behavior typically culminated with Dennis, unable to handle the bullying, lashing out at Nathan and other students with threatening words and physical attacks.

Addressing Bullying on a Schoolwide Front

One of my first actions was to speak with my administration and fellow staff members to ensure open communication and a common awareness that this issue was ongoing. The whole-school approach to dealing with bullying is often referred to in academic literature as the most effective way to prevent, intervene in, and respond to bullying episodes (Dake, Price, Telljohann, and Funk 2003). I knew for change to be successful it was necessary to get the entire school population involved with the strategies for change. In a staff meeting, bullying as a school problem was discussed and the progressive discipline policy was reviewed—but that did not feel sufficient. The policy had been in place previously and was not an effective tool; as a staff we committed to not only zero tolerance of bullying behaviors but zero tolerance of avoidance. We as a staff were not effectively modelling positive behaviors, as too often teachers would turn away from an incident or not take bullying seriously.

Staff members worked cohesively to reinforce the decision to address all incidents of bullying behavior, and the communication among staff members was greatly improved as a result. As a staff, we now had a more meaningful purpose on yard duty, as we knew which students to be attentive of and which students might need help. A message was sent to students that bullying behavior was unacceptable and that there would be consequences for bullying. We also had used a more meaningful system to record negative behaviors during recess breaks. For example, all yard-duty teachers had two-way radios to communicate with administration in the school as well as other staff spread across the school grounds; incident report forms that were used to track behaviors were shared among staff to communicate ongoing issues.

Taking Classroom Measures

Recognizing that something must be done to combat the bullying problem within my classroom, I utilized a multi-prong approach which took parts from various anti-bullying resources and information. I immediately altered my management plan to decrease opportunities for bullying to occur; this meant selective grouping, preferential seating, and more rules and policing of breaks (bathroom and fountain). In my own classroom, I also introduced restorative conferences as a way to replace the negative culture with one of respect, inclusion, responsibility, and accountability (Transforming Conflict 2001). Our conferences were scheduled weekly but sometimes occurred more often if the situation required it; similarly, mini-conferences might occur between select students, if necessary, outside of the class conference. Conferencing allowed students to practise their skills in speaking and listening as well as in problem solving. When a situation arose, we would discuss it in regard to three main questions:
- What happened?
- Who was involved or affected?
- What can we do differently in the future?

I found that if solutions were created cooperatively, the students were more likely to honor the solution or consequence given. For example, here's what happened in the case of Dennis and Nathan. The bullying behavior (teasing and taunting at recess) was discussed, and the two boys decided that Dennis would like to talk with Nathan and explain how he felt when Nathan bullied him; however, Dennis wanted to write it in a letter, so Nathan could not interrupt with excuses about his behavior. This conference was the first of several involving these two, but it laid the groundwork for future communication. Over time the issues became less frequent as the two boys began to respect and understand each other.

During classroom conferences, I also introduced focus lessons on bullying. We discussed the basics of bullying—what it is, what it feels like, and what the consequences of bullying are for everyone. We also talked about why people might bully and what targets of bullying can do. Some of the ideas we reviewed include these:
- telling the student who is bullying to stop (if the student feels safe to do so)
- removing yourself from the situation
- telling an adult what is happening
- refraining from using bullying behaviors while responding to a person who bullies

By establishing learning outcomes for my class, I was able to guide the instruction into areas in which students needed additional support and awareness. Using examples of common school issues and completing surveys on bullying in the classroom and school community, we were able to show that bullying can happen to anyone and that we need to develop a community where students and adults want the behavior to stop. I wanted to ensure that each student, especially targets of bullying, knew that it was not their fault and that they did not deserve to be treated this way.

Did I perfect a classroom against bullying? While that would be ideal, it is also naive to believe. But what I, with the support of my colleagues, was able to achieve was a marked improvement in the culture of the school and the actions of my 22 students. Moving from reactionary measures with a focus on punishment to a learning atmosphere with an emphasis on good citizenship and character education aided—and will continue to aid—in creating a safer school environment for all members of the community.

References:

Dake, J. A., J. H. Price, S. K. Telljohann, and J. B. Funk. 2003. "Teacher perceptions and practices regarding school bullying prevention." *Journal of School Health* 73 (9): 347–355.

Public Safety Canada. 2008. *First Steps to Stop Bullying: Adults Helping Children Aged 4 to 11.* Retrieved from http://www.publicsafety.gc.ca/res/cp/bully_4211-eng.aspx

Transforming Conflict. 2001. *Dealing with Bullying Using Restorative and Relational Strategies.* Retrieved from http://www.transformingconflict.org/Dealing_with_Bullying_using_Restorative_and_Relational_Strategies.html

Towards a Change in Headlines

As we put finishing touches to the manuscript of our book, tragic stories of bullycide—suicide brought on by bullying—have once again hit the news.

Debra Pepler, a professor in the Faculty of Health at York University, responded to the death of Mitchell Wilson, an 11-year-old boy with muscular dystrophy who killed himself rather than testify against the boy who bullied him. She reported that, even though Canada has an international reputation of being "nice" and dealing successfully with issues of diversity, inclusion, and equity, when it comes to our children, we are not keeping them safe well. Pepler writes, "We are not providing them with the necessary supports to learn how to live in healthy relationships." To her, bullying is not about punishment but about helping students understand the nature of power and the way that it plays out in children's lives.

The responsibility to address bullying can't fall on schools alone. In countries that have made progress in dealing with bullying, the initiative to look at the issue has been national. For instance, in the United States, President Barack Obama is hosting an anti-bullying conference and launching a website in response to a middle-school boy, Jamey Rodemeyer, killing himself over gay bullying. Jamey spoke openly to his parents about the bullying he endured as a sixth and seventh grader; in high school he had become more withdrawn. One of Jamey's last online messages is this: "I always say how bullied I am but no one listens." The hate messages the boy received are horrifying—for example, "I wouldn't care if he died. No one would. So just do it."

What makes someone so hateful? Who is confronting the bigots who are making life worse for kids like Jamey? Jamey's parents hope to make a difference. They are asking parents to get their children to talk about bullying and to find people that bullied students might talk to. In his newspaper column, Dan Savage (The It Gets Better Project) challenges us to join the Rodemeyers in their cause to do whatever is possible to stand up for others. Perhaps a donation is a place to start, Savage writes. And then? "Find something else you can do and go do it."

Then do more.

Bullying in all its forms is a horrific part of our culture. It probably will never be eliminated, and no book, program, or policy will eradicate the meanness and taunting that have targeted hundreds of thousands of youth. Celebrities such as Lady Gaga and activists like Dan Savage are making the plea to find ways to make harassment and cyber-harassment illegal. These hateful crimes should be investigated and prosecuted before a grieving family has to bury a child.

Not after.

We are sad that the headlines about bully incidents still haunt us. We are optimistic, however, that the classroom can be shaped in ways that provide support for all students no matter where their strengths lie, no matter how their differences manifest themselves, no matter where they come from and where they are going. We hope that we have given teachers creative, new ways to help their students communicate with one another. We trust that the suggested lessons and events will spark further ideas that help students collaborate and learn together. We hope that we have given enough ideas about how to lay the foundation so that students will build their lives in new ways—as compassionate individuals— caring about themselves, each other, and the work that lies before them.

It is our hope that this book will be used so that schools can be one of the main places where the bully issue is confronted effectively. We want schools to be environments where caring citizens are nurtured and where the students will ultimately change today's disturbing headlines into more positive ones.

Let us start by listening.

Appendix A

Recommended Resources on the Bully Issue

The wealth of resources on the bully issue has encouraged us to create this rather comprehensive listing which encompasses professional reading, scripts, chapter books, picture books, novels, anthologies, websites, and films.

Professional Reading

Aronson, Elliot. 2000. *Nobody Left to Hate: Teaching Compassion After Columbine*. New York: Henry Holt and Company.

Artz, Sibylle. 1998. *Sex, Power & the Violent Girl*. Toronto: Trifolium Books.

Atlas, R. S., and D. J. Pepler. 1998. "Observations of bullying in the classroom." *Journal of Educational Research* 92, 86–99.

Beane, Allan L. 2005. *The Bully Free Classroom*. Minneapolis, MN: Free Spirit Publishing.

Brownlie, Faye, and Judith King. 2011. *Learning in Safe Schools*, 2d ed. Markham: ON: Pembroke Publishers.

Coloroso, Barbara. 2002. *The Bully, the Bullied, and the Bystander*. New York: HarperCollins.

_____. 2005. *Just Because It's Not Wrong Doesn't Make It Right: From Toddlers to Teens, Teaching Kids to Think and Act Ethically*. Toronto: Viking.

_____. 2007. *Extraordinary Evil: A Brief History of Genocide*. Toronto: Viking.

Craig, Wendy, and Yossi Harel. 2004. "Bullying, physical fighting, and victimization." In *Young People's Health in Context: Health Behaviour in School-Aged Children (HSBC) Study: International Report from the 2001/2002 Survey* (Health Policy for Children and Adolescents, no. 4), edited by C. Currie, C. Roberts, A. Morgan, R. Smith, W. Settertobulte, O. Samdal, and V. Barnekow Rasmussen (pp. 133–144). Copenhagen, Denmark: World Health Organization.

Craig, Wendy, and Debra J. Pepler. 1997. "Observations of bullying and victimization in the schoolyard." *Canadian Journal of School Psychology* 13, 41–60.

Craig, Wendy, Debra J. Pepler, Jennifer Connolly, and Kathryn Henderson. 2007. "Towards a developmental perspective on victimization." In *Peer Harassment in School: The Plight of the Vulnerable and Victimized*, edited by J. Juvonen and S. Graham (pp. 242–262). New York: Guilford Press.

Fine, Esther Sokolov, Ann Lacey, and Joan Baer. 1995. *Children as Peacemakers*. Portsmouth, NH: Heinemann.

Galey, Paula. 2004. *Keep Cool! Strategies for Managing Anger at School*. Markham, ON: Pembroke Publishers.

Garbarino, James, and Ellen deLara. 2002. *And Words Can Hurt Forever: How to Protect Adolescents from Bullying, Harassment and Emotional Violence*. New York: Simon & Schuster.

Henkin, Roxanne. 2005. *Confronting Bullying: Literacy as a Tool for Character Education*. Portsmouth, NH: Heinemann.

Hinduja, Sameer, and Justin W. Patchin. 2008. *Bullying Beyond the Schoolyard: Preventing and Responding to Cyberbullying*. New York: Corwin Press.

Jacobs, Thomas A. 2010. *Teen Cyberbullying Investigated: Where Do Your Rights End and Consequences Begin?* Minneapolis, MN: Free Spirit Publishing.

Katch, Jane. 2003. *They Don't Like Me: Lessons on Bullying and Teasing from a Preschool Classroom*. Boston, MA: Beacon Press.

Linning, Lynn, Margaret Phillips, and Rayma Turton. 1997. *A Literature-Based Approach to Bullying*. Hamilton, Australia: The Literature Base Publications.

Lundy, Kathleen Gould. 2004. *What Do I Do About the Kid Who…?* Markham, ON: Pembroke Publishers.

_____. 2008. *Teaching Fairly in an Unfair World*. Markham, ON: Pembroke Publishers.

McNamara, B. E., and F. J. McNamara. 1997. *Keys to Dealing with Bullies*. Hauppage, NY: Barron's.

McQuade, Samuel C., James P. Colt, and Nancy Meyer. 2009. *Cyber Bullying: Protecting Kids & Adults from Online Bullies*. Westport, CT: Praeger.

Murphy, Ed, and Rob Lewers. 2000. *The Hidden Hurt.* Sydney, Australia: Wizard Books.

Myers, R. E. 2006. *Respect Matters.* Tucson, AZ: A Good Year Book.

Namie, Gary, and Ruth Namie. 2003. *The Bully at Work.* Naperville, IL: Sourcebooks.

O'Connell, Paul, Debra Pepler, and Wendy Craig. 1999. "Peer involvement in bullying: Insights and challenges." *Journal of Adolescence* 22, 437–452.

Paley, Vivian Gussey. 1992. *You Can't Say, You Can't Play.* Cambridge, MA: Harvard College.

Palomares, Susanna. 2001. *Lessons in Tolerance and Diversity.* Torrance, CA: Innerchoice Publishing.

Parsons, Les. 2005. *Bullied Teacher, Bullied Student.* Markham, ON: Pembroke Publishers.

Pepler, Debra J., and Wendy Craig. 2000. *Making a Difference in Bullying* (Report No. 60). Toronto: LaMarsh Centre for Research on Violence and Conflict Resolution, York University.

Rigby, Ken. 1998. *Bullying in Schools and What to Do About It.* Markham, ON: Pembroke Publishers.

_____. 2001. *Stop the Bullying: A Handbook for Teachers.* Markham, ON: Pembroke Publishers.

Ryan, Kevin, and Karen E. Bohlin. 1999. *Building Character in Schools.* San Francisco, CA: Jossey-Bass.

Shariff, Shaheen. 2009. *Confronting Cyber-Bullying: What Schools Need to Know to Control Misconduct and Avoid Legal Consequences.* Cambridge, MA: Cambridge University Press.

Simmonds, Jennifer. 2003. *Seeing Red: An Anger Management and Peacemaking Curriculum for Kids.* Minneapolis, MN: New Society Publishers.

Simmons, Rachel. 2002. *Odd Girl Out: The Hidden Culture of Aggression in Girls.* Orlando, FL: Harcourt.

Sullivan, Keith. 2000. *The Anti-Bullying Book.* Auckland, NZ: Oxford.

Stones, Rosemary. 1993. *Don't Pick on Me: How to Handle Bullying.* Markham, ON: Pembroke Publishers.

Swartz, Larry, ed. 2004. The Bully Issue. *Orbit* 34, no. 2 [published by OISE/UT].

Swartz, Larry, and Debbie Nyman. 2010. *Drama Schemes, Themes & Dreams.* Markham, ON: Pembroke Publishers.

Thompson, Michael, and Catherine O'Neill Grace. 2001. *Best Friends, Worst Enemies: Understanding the Social Lives of Children.* New York: Ballantyne Books.

Willard, Nancy E. 2007. *Cyber-Safe Kids, Cyber-Safe Teens: Helping Young People Learn to Use the Internet Safely and Responsibly.* San Francisco, CA: Jossey-Bass.

Wiseman, Rosalind. 2002. *Queen Bees & Wannabes.* New York: Three Rivers Press.

Zarzour, Kim. 1999. *The Schoolyard Bully.* New York: HarperCollins.

References for Students

Alexander, Jenny. 2003. *Bullies, Bigmouths & So-called Friends.*

Cohen-Posey, Kate. 1995. *How to Handle Bullies, Teasers and Other Meanies.*

Elliott, Michelle. 2005. *Bullying.*

Gardner, Olivia. 2008. *Letters to a Bullied Girl: Messages of Healing and Hope.*

Humans, Jackie (Illus. Nikki Lee). 2011. *15 Ways to Zap a Bully.*

Johnson, Julie. 1998. *How Do I Feel About … Bullies and Gangs.*

Karres, Erika V. Shearin. 2004. *Mean Chicks, Clicks, and Dirty Tricks.*

Kelly, Megan, and Carrie Jones, eds. 2011. *Dear Bully: Seventy Authors Tell Their Stories.*

Ludwig, Trudy (Illus. Beth Adams). 2010. *Confessions of a Former Bully.*

Ragona, Sandy, and Kerri Pentel. 2004. *Eliminate Bullying.*

Scott-Norman, Fiona, ed. 2011. *Don't Peak at High School.*

Shapiro, Ouisie. 2010. *Bullying and Me: Schoolyard Stories.*

Simmons, Rachel. 2004. *Odd Girl Speaks Out.*

Slavens, Elaine (Illus. Brooke Kerrigan). 2003. *Bullying: Deal with It Before Push Comes to Shove.*

Stones, Rosemary. 1993. *Don't Pick on Me: How to Handle Bullying.*

Yee, J. W. 1997. *The Bully Buster Book.*

Zerner, Sandra. 2011. *It's Good 2B Good: Why It's Not Bad to Be Good.*

Scripts

Brooks, Martha, and Maureen Hunter. 1995. *I Met a Bully on the Hill.*

Foon, Dennis. 1993. *Seesaw.*

Gotlib, Alan, and Alice Brass. 1997. *"B" Is for Bully.*

McCleod, Joan. 2002. *The Shape of a Girl.*

More Than a Play. 2010. [Elementary Teachers' Federation of Ontario].

Picture Books for Readers, Ages 5 to 7

Agassi, Martine. 2000. *Hands Are Not for Hitting.*

Alexander, Martha. 2001. *I Sure Am Glad to See You, Blackboard Bear.*

Bateman, Teresa (Illus. Jackie Urbanovic). 2004. *The Bully Blockers Club.*

Berenstain, Stan, and Jan Berenstain. 1993. *The Berenstain Bears and the Bully.*

Carlson, Nancy. 1983. *Loudmouth George and the Sixth-Grade Bully.*

Cook, Julia (Illus. Anita DuFalla). 2009. *Bully B.E.A.N.S.*

Cosby, Bill (Illus. Varnette P. Honeywood). 1997. *The Meanest Thing to Say.*

Cox, Phil Roxbee (Illus. Jan McCafferty). 2004. *Don't Be a Bully, Billy.*

dePaola, Tomie. 1979. *Oliver Button Is a Sissy.*

Lalli, Judy. 1996. *Make Someone Smile … and 40 More Ways to Be a Peaceful Person.*

Mayer, Gina, and Mercer Mayer. 1999. *Just a Bully.*

Slater, Teddy (Illus. Pat Porter). 1995. *Who's Afraid of the Big Bad Bully?*

Thomas, Pat. 2000. *Stop Picking on Me: A First Look at Bullying.*

Verdick, Elizabeth (Illus. Elizabeth Verdick). 2004. *Words Are Not for Hurting.*

Picture Books for the Teacher to Read Aloud

Alexander, Claire. 2008. *Lucy and the Bully.*

Browne, Anthony. 1985. *Willy the Champ* (Also: *Willy the Wimp, Willy and Hugh*).

Bunting, Eve (Illus. David Frampton). 2001. *Riding the Tiger.*

Cannon, Janell. 2000. *Crickwing.*

Carlson, Nancy. 2000. *Henry and the Bully.*

Casley, Judith. 2001. *Bully.*

Choi, Yangsook. 2003. *The Name Jar.*

Cuyler, Margery (Illus. Arthur Howard). 2009. *Bullies Never Win.*

Goffe, Toni. 1991. *Bully for You.*

Gray, Kes (Illus. Lee Wildish). 2011. *Leave Me Alone.*

Hole, Stian. 2009. *Garmann's Street.*

Kristiansson, Leif. 2006. *Not My Fault.*

Kroll, Steven (Illus. Vincent Nguyen). 2006. *Jungle Bullies.*

Lester, Helen (Illus. Lynn Munsinger). 1999. *Hooway for Wodney Wat.*

Lovell, Patty (Illus. David Catrow). 2001. *Stand Tall, Molly Lou Melon.*

Ludwig, Trudy. 2005. *My Secret Bully.* (Also: *Just Kidding; Trouble Talk*)

McCain, Becky Ray (Illus. Todd Leonardo). 2001. *Nobody Knew What to Do: A Story About Bullying.*

Mobin-Uddin, Asma (Illus. Barbara Kiwak). 2005. *My Name Is Bilal.*

Moss, Marissa. 2006. *Amelia's Bully Survival Guide.*

Moss, Peggy (Illus. Lea Lyon). 2004. *Say Something.*

Moss, Peggy, and Dee Dee Tardif (Illus. Imre Geis). 2007. *Our Friendship Rules.*

Munson, Derek (Illus. Tara Calahan King). 2001. *Enemy Pie.*

Nickle, John. 1999. *The Ant Bully.*

O'Neill, Alexis (Illus. Larua Huliska-Beith). 2002. *The Recess Queen.*

Polacco, Patricia. 2001. *Mr. Lincoln's Way.* (Also: *Thank You, Mr. Falker*).

Peters, Andrew Fusek (Illus. Anna Wadham). 2007. *The Ant and the Big Bad Billy Goat.*

Rosenberg, Liz (Illus. Stephen Gammell). 1993. *Monster Mama.*

Ross, Tony. 2004. *Is It Because?*

Sadu, Itah. 1992. *Name Calling.*

Sesskin, Steve, and Allen Shamblin (Illus. Glin Dibley). 2002. *Don't Laugh at Me.*

Wishinsky, Frieda (Illus. Dean Griffiths). 2001. *Give Maggie a Chance.*

_____. (Illus. Kady MacDonald Denton). 2010. *You're Mean, Lily Jean.*

Chapter Books

Clements, Andrew. 2001. *Jake Drake: Bully Buster.*

Edwards, Michelle. 2005. *Stinky Stern Forever.*

Hogg, Gary. 1998. *Scrambled Eggs and Spider Legs.*

Howe, James (Illus. Melissa Sweet). 1996. *Pinky and Rex and the Bully.*

Richards, N. W. 2006. *How to Tame a Bully.*

Van Drannen, Wendelin. 2004. *Shredderman: Secret Identity.*

Wishinsky, Frieda. 2000. *So Long, Stinky Queen.*

Novels for Readers, Ages 8 to 12

Chan, Marty. 2010. *The Mystery of the Cyber Bully.*

Fine, Anne. 1993. *The Angel of Nitshill Road.*

Gates, Susan. 2000. *Raider.*

Katz, Farley. 2011. *Journal of a Schoolyard Bully: Notes on Noogies, Wet Willies and Wedgies.*

Langan, Paul. 2002. *The Bully.*

Lekich, John. 2002. *The Losers' Club.*

Paterson, Katherine. 2001. *The Field of Dogs.*

Roy, James. 2009. *Max Quigley, Technically Not a Bully.*

Sachs, Marilyn. 1968/1995. *Veronica Ganz.*
Spinelli, Jerry. 2002. *Loser.*
Stolz, Mary. 1963. *The Bully of Barkham Street.*
Tolan, Stephanie S. 2002. *Surviving the Applewhites.*

Novels for Young Adolescents

Almond, David (Illus. Dave McKean). 2008. *The Savage.*
Bloor, Edward. 1997. *Tangerine.*
Chambers, Aidan. 1985. *The Present Takers.*
Flake, Sharon G. 1988. *The Skin I'm In.*
Foon, Dennis. 2003. *Skud.*
Gardner, Graham. 2004. *Inventing Elliot.*
Howe, James. 2001. *The Misfits.*
Koss, Amy Goldman. 2006. *Poison Ivy: 3 Bullies, 2 Boyfriends, 1 Trial.*
MacLean, Jill. 2010. *Home Truths.*
Masters, Anthony. 1995. *Bullies Don't Hurt.*
Peters, Julie Anne. 2000. *Define "Normal."*
Pignat, Caroline. 2008. *Egghead.*
Prose, Francine. 2007. *Bullyville.*
Shulman, Mark. 2010. *Scrawl.*
Singer, Nicky. 2002. *Feather Boy.*
Strasser, Todd. 2000. *Give a Boy a Gun.*
Vansickle, Vikki. 2010. *Words That Start with B.*

Anthologies

Booth, David, ed. 2007. *Stand Tall.*
Ellis, Deborah, ed. 2010. *We Want You to Know.*
Fearnly, Fran, ed. 2004. *I Wrote on All Four Walls: Teens Speak Out About Violence.*
Green, Joan, and Kathy Lundy, eds. 2010. *No Bullies Allowed.*
Porter, Helen Carmichael. 2006. *The Bully and Me: Stories That Break the Cycle of Torment.*
Swartz, Larry, and Kathy Broad, eds. 2004. *Sticks and Stones.*

Films

It's a Girl's World (National Film Board).
Big Bully.
Bully Dance (National Film Board).
Mean Girls.
The Chorus (Les Choristes).
Finding Kind.

Websites

Focus on Bullying and on Harassment and Intimidation:
www.bced.gov.bc.ca/sco/resources.htm
Responding to Bullying in Secondary School Communities:
www.bced.gov.bc.ca/sco/resources.htm
Bully Online:
www.bullyonline.org
The Canadian Safe School Network:
www.cssn.org
The BC Safe Schools Communities Centre:
Info.safeschools@gems5gov.bc.ca
Safe, Caring and Orderly Schools: Ministry of Education, British Columbia:
www.bced.gov.bc.ca/sco/resources.htm
Barbara Coloroso:
www.kidsareworthit.com
Don't Laugh at Me:
www.dontlaugh.org
Cyberbullying:
www.cyberbullying.ca

Appendix B

Recommended Professional Resources

Books

Chambers, Aidan. 1993. *Tell Me: Children, Reading, and Talk*. Markham, ON: Pembroke Publishers.

Dunn, Sonja. 1999. *All Together Now: 200 of Sonja Dunn's Best Chants*. Markham, ON: Pembroke Publishers.

Gibbs, Jeanne. 2006. *Reaching All by Creating Tribes*, 30th anniversary edition. Windsor, CA: CenterSource Systems. (Also: *Discovering Gifts in Middle School*; *Learning in a Caring Culture Called Tribes*.)

Glass, Jennifer, Joan Green, and Kathleen Gould Lundy. 2011. *Talking to Learn: 50 Strategies for Developing Oral Language*. Don Mills, ON: Oxford University Press.

Gregory, T. B., and G. R. Smith. 1987. *High Schools as Communities: The Small School Reconsidered*. Bloomington, IN: Phi Delta Kappa.

Johnson, D. W., and R. T. Johnson. 1998. *Learning Together and Alone: Cooperative, Competitive and Individualistic Learning*, 5th edition. Englewood Cliffs, NJ: Allyn & Bacon.

Lundy, Kathleen Gould. 2004. *What Do I Do About the Kid Who...?* Markham, ON: Pembroke Publishers.

_____. 2007. *Leap into Literacy*. Markham, ON: Pembroke Publishers.

_____. 2008. *Teaching Fairly in an Unfair World*. Markham, ON: Pembroke Publishers.

Paley, V. G. 2010. *The Boy on the Beach: Building Community Through Play*. Chicago, IL: The University of Chicago Press.

Paterson, Kathy. 2007. *3-Minute Motivators*. Markham, ON: Pembroke Publishers.

Rolheiser, Carol, Mark Evans, and Mira Gambhir, eds. 2011. *Inquiry into Practice: Reaching Every Student Through Inclusive Curriculum*. Toronto: Ontario Institute for Studies in Education, University of Toronto.

Rose, Mike. 2009. *Why School?: Reclaiming Education for All of Us*. New York: The New Press.

Spence, Christopher M. 2009. *Achieving, Believing, and Caring*. Markham, ON: Pembroke Publishers.

Swartz, Larry, and Debbie Nyman. 2010. *Drama Schemes, Themes and Dreams*. Markham, ON: Pembroke Publishers.

Professional Development: Films Featuring Teachers

Children Full of Life
The Class
Etre et Avoir (To Be and To Have)
School Play
A Touch of Greatness
Yellow Brick Road
Based on a True Story
Chalk
Coach Carter
Dangerous Minds
Freedom Writers
The Miracle Worker
Temple Grandin
Blackboards
The Chorus (Les Choristes)
The History Boys
Mr. Holland's Opus
Mona Lisa Smile
The Prime of Miss Jean Brodie

Alphabet Grid

Use this grid for basic brainstorming.

a	b	c	d
e	f	g	h
i	j	k	l
m	n	o	p
q	r	s	t
u	v	w	x
y	z		

Caring Classroom A B C

a	b	c	d
acceptance	belonging	caring	dynamic
e	**f**	**g**	**h**
equality	fun	groups	harmony
i	**j**	**k**	**l**
inquiry	justice	kindness	listening
m	**n**	**o**	**p**
meetings	negotiation	order	perseverance
q	**r**	**s**	**t**
questions	respect	safety	trust
u	**v**	**w**	**x**
understanding	voice	welcome	eXtra special
y	**z**		
yes!	zero tolerance for bullying		

Pembroke Publishers © 2011 *Creating Caring Classrooms* by Kathleen Gould Lundy and Larry Swartz   ISBN 978-1-55138-270-8

A Triangle, a Square, and a Circle

Consider the relationships between someone who is bullied, someone who bullies, and someone who watches an incident of bullying happen. Now, cut these geometric shapes out and then explore how to place them in order to reflect your understanding.

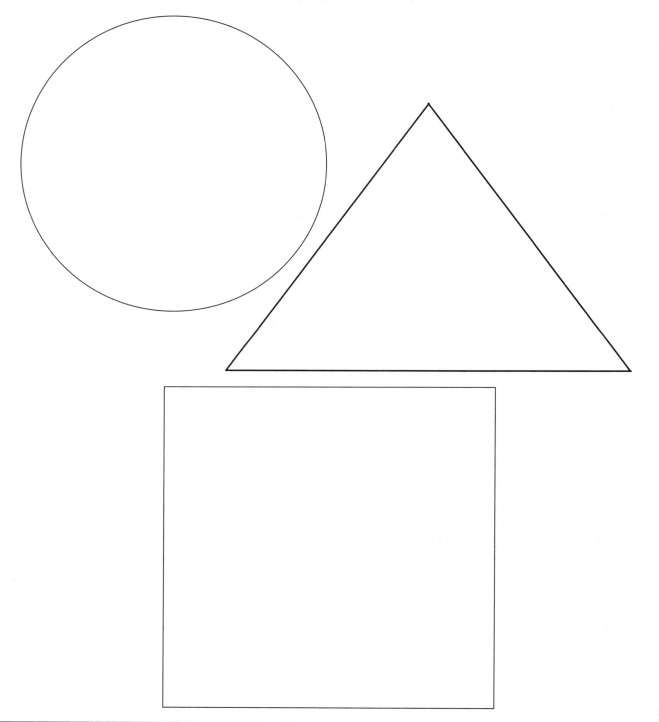

Pembroke Publishers © 2011 *Creating Caring Classrooms* by Kathleen Gould Lundy and Larry Swartz   ISBN 978-1-55138-270-8

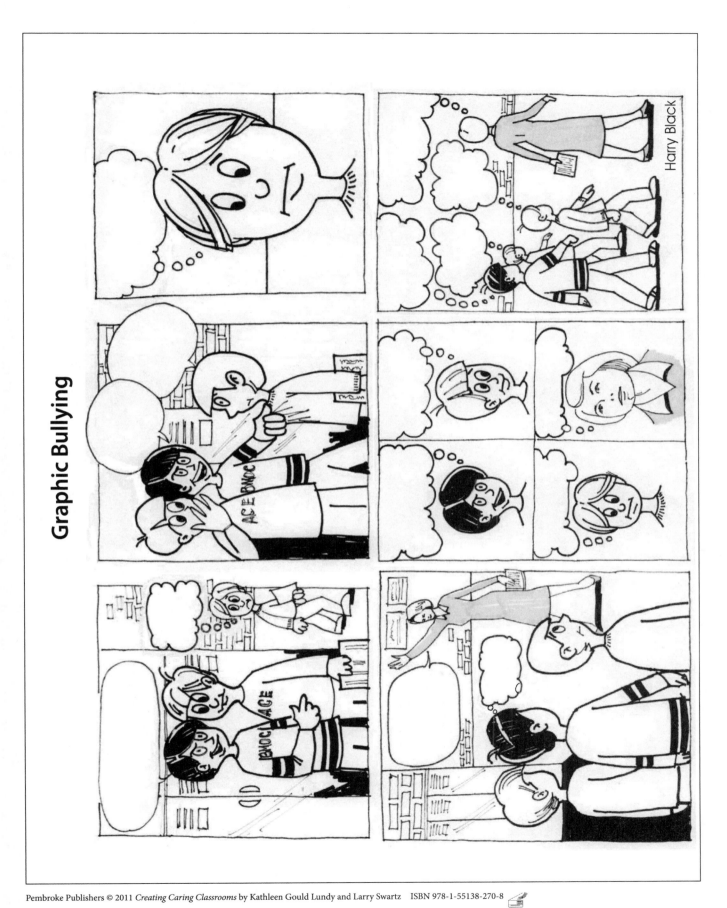

Index